Seven Steps to Getting a Job Fast

Michael Farr

Seven Steps to Getting a Job Fast

© 2002 by JIST Publishing, Inc.

Published by JIST Works, an imprint of JIST Publishing, Inc.
8902 Otis Avenue
Indianapolis, IN 46216-1033
Phone: 1-800-648-JIST   Fax: 1-800-JIST-FAX
E-mail: info@jist.com   Web site: www.jist.com

Visit **www.jist.com**. Come to our Web site for information on JIST, free job search information, and ordering information on our many products!

Quantity discounts are available for JIST books. Please call our Sales Department at 1-800-648-5478 for a free catalog and more information.

Printed in Canada
06 05 04 03   9 8 7 6 5 4 3 2

We have been careful to provide accurate information in this book, but it is possible that errors and omissions have been introduced. Please consider this in making any career plans or other important decisions. Trust your own judgment above all else and in all things.

Editor: Mary Ellen Stephenson
Interior Designer: Aleata Howard
Page Layout Coordinator: Carolyn J. Newland
Cover Designer: Nick Anderson
Proofreader: Jeanne Clark
Indexer: Tina Trettin

ISBN 1-56370-888-4

This Book Is Short, But It May Be All You Need

Compared to many job search books, this is a short book. I set out to make it that way, by covering only those things I have found would make the most difference to you in getting a good job in less time.

You could read parts of this book in a morning and conduct a more effective job search that same afternoon. Completing the worksheets and other activities (like writing a resume) would take more time, of course—but most people should be able to complete this book in a day or less. And you may find that this is all you need.

While career planning and job search can become complicated, here are a few simple truths:

1. If you will work, you might as well look for work you enjoy doing and are good at.

2. If you are going to look for a job, you might as well use methods that are likely to reduce the time it takes to find one.

These are the things I emphasize in this book. Of course, there is more to know about career planning, but this book covers the basics. If you use the techniques—and not just read about them—the odds are good that you will reduce the time it takes to find your next job. And you will be more likely to find a better job than you might have otherwise.

I wish you well.

Mike Farr

Acknowledgments

The more you give away, the more you get back in return…

I don't know where to begin thanking everyone who has helped me over the years, but here is a start:

My Mom: *Born in 1908, Anna is 94 years young now and doing just fine. I love her dearly, and she continues to inspire me. She is personally responsible for rearranging my books face out in bookstores throughout southwest Florida, should you ever wonder about that.*

My Dad: *He modeled the work ethic I have, and the persistence (there were five kids in the family…). He retired after 29 years with the same employer, a remarkable record by today's standards. Thanks for being there. Oh, I'm sorry for all the trouble I caused you as a teenager…*

Sister William Mary: *My teacher in grades 5, 6, 7, and 8. She and others taught me how to write and think. Thanks for being a good teacher.*

A.J. Nania: *My freshman-year English professor at Notre Dame. He taught me to write things short and long and to understand eighth grade grammar. Short is harder, I learned, and takes longer per page. A great teacher.*

Sandra: *We've been married more than 30 years now, and she's been there through all my career changes and most of my life. I still like spending time with her, can you imagine? Thanks for everything.*

My family: *I am blessed with two great kids, two brothers, two sisters, aunts and uncles, nieces and nephews, lots of cousins. Wish they all lived closer.*

Everyone else: *I have a very long list of people who have helped me along the way, including good friends, the good people I work with, the many job seekers whom I have learned so much from, and so many others.*

Thanks.

Table of Contents

A Brief Introduction to Using This Book

Why does it take some people more time than others to find a job? And what sort of job should you be looking for?

The answers to these questions will require you to learn something about career planning and job seeking. But you can't just read about getting a job. Job seeking requires action, and the most effective action is to go out and make contacts with the people who are most likely to need someone with your skills. And the best way to do *that* is to make a job out of getting a job.

This may sound simple, but doing it well requires some preparation. After many years of experience, I have identified just seven basic things that make a big difference in your job search. Each will be covered and expanded on in this book. These steps are

1. **IDENTIFY YOUR KEY SKILLS.**
    Most people can't explain what they are good at or what they like to do. Spending some time to clarify this will help you in so many ways, in your job search and in your life.

2. **DEFINE YOUR IDEAL JOB.**
    Too many people look for "a" job without knowing what "THE" job would be. So I encourage you to define your ideal position, knowing you can always compromise later.

3. **LEARN THE MOST EFFECTIVE JOB SEARCH METHODS.**
    Once you know what you are looking for, you need to know what job search methods are most likely to help you find it.

4. **WRITE A SUPERIOR RESUME.**
    Most people spend too much time worrying about their resume. Instead, you will learn to write an acceptable resume in just an hour or so and then a better one later, if you need one.

5. **ORGANIZE YOUR TIME TO GET 2 INTERVIEWS A DAY.**
    Yes, it's possible to get 2 interviews a day—if you know how to do it.

6. **DRAMATICALLY IMPROVE YOUR INTERVIEWING SKILLS.**
   Just an hour or so spent reading this section of the book can make a big difference in how well you handle your next interview. What you learn could, indeed, increase your earnings a thousand dollars or more.

7. **FOLLOW UP ON ALL JOB LEADS.**
   Doing this well often makes the difference in who gets the job and who continues to wait for an offer.

Of Course, You Can't Just Read About It...

As I said earlier, to get results you will have to actively apply what you learn in this book. One of the biggest reasons some people stay unemployed longer than others do is that they sit at home waiting for someone to knock on their door, call them up, or make them an offer via e-mail. That passive approach too often results in their waiting and waiting, while others are out there getting the offers.

So, Trust Me—Do the Worksheets

I know you will resist completing the worksheets. But, trust me—they are worth your time. Doing them will give you a better sense of what you are good at, what you want to do, and how to go about doing it. Spending some time to learn career planning and job seeking methods will likely result in your getting more interviews. And, you will present yourself better in those interviews. Is this worth giving up a night of TV? Yes, I think so.

The interesting thing is that, once you finish this book and its activities, you will have spent more time planning your career than most people do. And you will know more than the average job seeker about finding a job.

> ## Quip
>
> *Good news for those who do their homework.*
>
> Most people spend more time watching TV each week than they spend on career planning in an entire year. Fewer than 10 percent of all job seekers have even read a book on job seeking. While this lack of preparation is a big problem for them, it is good news for you. Knowing even a little more than the next person can give you a big advantage in the job search and in life.

Why This Is a Short Book

I've taught job seeking skills for many years, and I've written longer and more detailed books than this one. Yet I have often been asked to tell someone, in a few minutes or hours, the most important things they should do in their career planning or job search. Instructors and counselors also ask the same question because they have only a short time to spend with the folks they're trying to help.

I've thought about what is most important to know, if time is short. The seven topics covered in this book are the ones I think are the most important to know. This book is short enough that you can scan it in a morning and conduct a more effective job search that afternoon. Doing all the activities would take more time but would prepare you far better. Of course, you can learn more about all of the topics *Seven Steps* covers, but this book may be all that you need.

Identify Your Key Skills—and Develop a Powerful New "Skills Language" to Describe Yourself

One employer survey found that most people interviewed by the employers did not present the skills they had to do the jobs they sought. Job applicants could not, for example, answer the basic question "Why should I hire you?"

So, if you want to do well in interviews, it is essential that you be able to describe what you are good at and why you think you can do the job. This same knowledge is important in deciding what type of job you will enjoy and do well. For these reasons, I consider identifying your skills a necessary part of a successful career plan or job search.

Quip

We all have thousands of skills.

Consider the many skills required to do even a simple thing like ride a bike or bake a cake. But, of all the skills you have, employers want to know those key skills you have for the job they need done. You must clearly identify these key skills and then emphasize them in interviews. The section that follows will help you identify these skills.

There Are Three Types of Skills

Most people think of their "skills" as job-related skills, such as using a computer. But we all have other types of skills that are important for success on a job—and that are important to employers. The triangle on page 5 presents skills in three groups, and I think that this is a very useful way to consider skills for our purposes.

Let's review these three types of skills—self-management, transferable, and job-related—and identify those that are most important to you.

Self-Management Skills

Below, write three things about yourself that you think make you a good worker. Pick the first three things that come to mind.

YOUR "GOOD WORKER" TRAITS

1. _____

2. _____

3. _____

You just wrote what are among the most important things for an employer to know about you. They describe your basic personality and your ability to adapt to new environments. They are among the most important skills to emphasize in interviews, yet most job seekers don't realize the importance of these skills—and don't mention them.

SELF-MANAGEMENT SKILLS CHECKLIST

Review the skills list that follows and put a check mark beside each skill you have. The key self-management skills listed first are those employers find particularly important. If one or more of these key skills apply to you, mentioning them in interviews can help you greatly.

Key Self-Management Skills—
Employers Value These Highly

_____ accept supervision		_____ hard worker	
_____ get along with coworkers		_____ honest	
_____ get things done on time		_____ productive	
_____ good attendance		_____ punctual	

Other Self-Management Skills

_____ able to coordinate		_____ good-natured	
_____ ambitious		_____ helpful	
_____ assertive		_____ humble	
_____ capable		_____ imaginative	
_____ cheerful		_____ independent	
_____ competent		_____ industrious	
_____ complete assignments		_____ informal	
_____ conscientious		_____ intelligent	
_____ creative		_____ intuitive	
_____ dependable		_____ learn quickly	
_____ discreet		_____ loyal	
_____ eager		_____ mature	
_____ efficient		_____ methodical	
_____ energetic		_____ modest	
_____ enthusiastic		_____ motivated	
_____ expressive		_____ natural	
_____ flexible		_____ open-minded	
_____ formal		_____ optimistic	
_____ friendly		_____ original	

(continues)

(continued)

_____ patient	_____ solve problems
_____ persistent	_____ spontaneous
_____ physically strong	_____ steady
_____ practice new skills	_____ tactful
_____ reliable	_____ take pride in work
_____ resourceful	_____ tenacious
_____ responsible	_____ thrifty
_____ self-confident	_____ trustworthy
_____ sense of humor	_____ versatile
_____ sincere	_____ well organized

List Your Other Self-Management Skills

_____

_____

_____

After you have completed the checklist, circle the five self-management skills you think are most important to use in your next job and list them in the box that follows.

YOUR TOP FIVE SELF-MANAGEMENT SKILLS

1. _____

2. _____

3. _____

4. _____

5. _____

Transferable Skills

We all have skills that can be transferred from one job or career to another. For example, the ability to organize events could be used in a variety of jobs and might be essential for success in certain occupations. Your mission is to find a job that requires the skills you have and enjoy using.

TRANSFERABLE SKILLS CHECKLIST

Put a check mark beside the each of the skills you have that are listed below. You may have used them in a previous job or in some non-work setting.

Key Transferable Skills—Employers Value These Highly

_____	computer skills	_____	meet deadlines
_____	instruct others	_____	meet the public
_____	negotiate	_____	organize/manage projects
_____	manage money, budgets	_____	public speaking
_____	manage people	_____	written communication

Skills for Working with Things

_____	assemble things	_____	observe/inspect things
_____	build things	_____	operate tools, machines
_____	construct/repair things	_____	repair things
_____	drive, operate vehicles	_____	use complex equipment
_____	good with hands	_____	use computers

(continues)

(continued)

Skills for Working with Data

_____ analyze data

_____ audit records

_____ budget

_____ calculate/compute

_____ check for accuracy

_____ classify things

_____ compare

_____ compile

_____ count

_____ detail-oriented

_____ evaluate

_____ find information on the Internet

_____ investigate

_____ keep financial records

_____ locate information

_____ manage money

_____ observe/inspect

_____ record facts

_____ research

_____ set up or analyze spreadsheets

_____ synthesize

_____ take inventory

_____ use database, financial, or related software

Skills for Working with People

_____ administer

_____ advise

_____ care for

_____ coach

_____ confront others

_____ counsel people

_____ demonstrate

_____ diplomatic

_____ help others

_____ instruct

_____ interview people

_____ kind

_____ listen

_____ negotiate

_____ outgoing

_____ patient

_____ perceptive

_____ persuade

_____ pleasant

_____ sensitive

_____ sociable

_____ supervise

_____ tactful

_____ tolerant

_____ tough

_____ trusting

_____ understanding

Skills for Working with Words and Ideas

_____ articulate

_____ communicate verbally

_____ correspond with others

_____ create new ideas

_____ design

_____ edit

_____ ingenious

_____ inventive

_____ library or Internet research

_____ logical

_____ public speaking

_____ remember information

_____ use word-processing software

_____ write clearly

Leadership Skills

_____ arrange social functions

_____ competitive

_____ decisive

_____ delegate

_____ direct others

_____ explain things to others

_____ influence others

_____ initiate new tasks

_____ make decisions

_____ manage or direct others

_____ mediate problems

_____ motivate people

_____ negotiate agreements

_____ plan events

_____ results-oriented

_____ risk-taker

_____ run meetings

_____ self-confident

_____ self-motivate

_____ solve problems

(continues)

(continued)

Creative and Artistic Skills

_____ artistic

_____ compose music scores or songs

_____ dance, body movement

_____ drawing, art

_____ expressive

_____ perform, act

_____ play musical instrument

_____ present artistic ideas

_____ use graphic design software

_____ write fiction or creative writing

List Your Other Transferable Skills

_____

_____

_____

When you are finished, circle the five transferable skills you feel are most important for you to use in your next job and list them in the box below.

YOUR TOP FIVE TRANSFERABLE SKILLS

1. _____

2. _____

3. _____

4. _____

5. _____

Job-Related Skills

Job-related skills are those you need to do a particular occupation. A carpenter, for example, needs to know how to use various tools. Before you select your job-related skills to emphasize, you must first have a clear idea of the jobs you want. So let's put off developing your job-related skills checklist until after you have defined the job you want. That topic is covered next.

Complete the worksheet that follows after you have read "Step 2: Set a Specific Job Objective Before You Go Looking."

Quip

Too good to be true?

Most people say that taking inventory of their skills and activities made them feel good; some say working through the checklists was one of the best things they have ever done. If you do it right, you are telling the truth about what you are good at. It's okay to tell the truth, even if it makes you sound good. Using your new "skills language" may be uncomfortable at first, but this information is what employers need to know about you in an interview.

YOUR TOP FIVE JOB-RELATED SKILLS

1. _____

2. _____

3. _____

4. _____

5. _____

Set a Specific Job Objective Before You Go Looking

Too many people look for a job without clearly knowing what they are looking for. So, before you go out looking for *a* job, you should first define exactly what you want—*THE* job, not *a* job.

Most people think that a job objective is the same as a job title, but it isn't. You need to consider other elements of what makes a job satisfying for you. Then, later, you can decide what that job is called—its title—and what industry it might be in.

DEFINE YOUR IDEAL JOB NOW— YOU CAN ALWAYS COMPROMISE ON IT LATER...

There are many things to consider in defining the ideal job for you. The eight questions that follow will help you consider things that are often important in defining a position that satisfies you fully. Once you have considered your answers, your task then becomes finding a position that is as close to your ideal job as possible.

1. **What skills do you want to use?**

    From the skills lists in Step 1, select the top five skills that you enjoy using and most want to use in your next job.

    _____

    _____

    _____

    _____

    _____

(continues)

(continued)

2. What type of special knowledge do you have?

Perhaps you know how to fix radios, keep accounting records, or cook food. Write down the things you know from schooling, training, hobbies, family experiences, and other sources. One or more of these knowledges could make you a very special applicant in the right setting. _____

_____

_____

_____

_____

_____

3. With what types of people do you prefer to work?

Do you like to work in competition with others, or do you prefer hardworking folks, creative personalities, or some other types? _____

_____

_____

_____

_____

_____

4. What type of work environment do you prefer?

Do you want to work inside, outside, in a quiet place, a busy place, a clean place, or have a window with a nice view? List the types of environments that are most important to you.

_____

_____

_____

_____

_____

5. **Where do you want your next job to be located—in what city or region?**

Near a bus line? Close to a childcare center? Near your mom? If you are open to living and working anywhere, what would your ideal community be like? _____

_____

_____

_____

_____

_____

6. **How much money do you hope to make in your next job?**

Many people will take less money if they like a job in other ways—or if they quickly need a job to survive. Think about the minimum you would take as well as what you would eventually like to earn. Your next job will probably pay somewhere in between. What benefits would you like to receive?

_____

_____

_____

_____

_____

7. **How much and what types of responsibility are you willing to accept?**

Usually, the more money you want to make, the more responsibility you must accept. Do you want to work by yourself, be part of a group, or be in charge? If so, at what level?

_____

_____

(continues)

(continued)

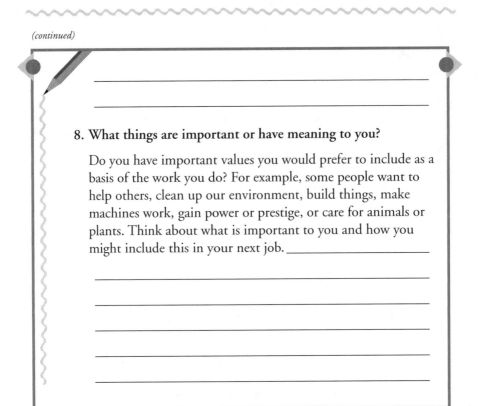

8. **What things are important or have meaning to you?**

Do you have important values you would prefer to include as a basis of the work you do? For example, some people want to help others, clean up our environment, build things, make machines work, gain power or prestige, or care for animals or plants. Think about what is important to you and how you might include this in your next job. _____

_____

_____

_____

_____

_____

Is It Possible to Find Your Ideal Job?

Can you find a job that meets all the criteria you just defined? Perhaps. Some people do. The harder you look, the more likely you are to find it.

But, you will likely need to compromise on some criteria, so it is useful to know what is *most* important to include in your next job. Go back over your responses to the eight questions and mark those few things that you would most like to have or include in your ideal job. Then write a brief outline of this ideal job in the following box. Don't worry about a job title, whether you have the experience, or other practical matters yet.

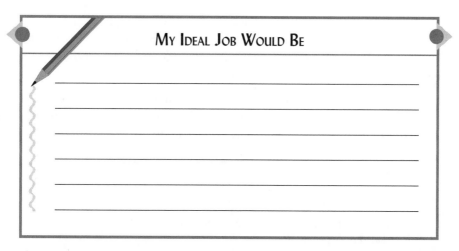

MY IDEAL JOB WOULD BE

How to Explore Specific Job Titles and Industries

You might find your ideal job in an occupation you haven't considered. And, even if you are sure of the occupation you want, it may be in an industry that you're not familiar with. This combination of occupation and industry forms the basis for your job search, and you should explore a variety of options.

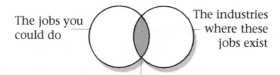

The jobs you could do

The industries where these jobs exist

Your ideal job exists in the overlap of those jobs that interest you most *and* in those industries that best meet your needs and interests!

Explore More Than 250 Specific Job Titles

Your ideal job has a variety of characteristics, but it does not yet have a job title. The reason is that some of the things you want, such as a specific work environment, can be found in many jobs and in many industries. But, to conduct an effective job search, it is helpful to limit your search to a range of jobs most likely to match your ideal.

The most-often-used source of information on jobs is a book titled the *Occupational Outlook Handbook (OOH),* published by the U.S. Department of Labor. The list that follows presents 264 job titles from the *OOH,* covering more than 85% of the U.S. workforce.

You can simply find a job title that interests you and then get additional information on it from the *OOH.* The descriptions provide details on earnings, education or training required, skills and abilities needed, working conditions, related jobs, sources of additional information (including Internet sources), and other particulars.

A sample job description from the Occupational Outlook Handbook is included in Appendix B.

Most libraries and bookstores will have a copy of the *Occupational Outlook Handbook* or of another book with the same information, titled *America's Top 300 Jobs.* You can also get *OOH* job descriptions on the Internet at www.bls.gov/oco/home.htm or at www.CareerOINK.com.

A simple but effective way to explore job alternatives is to go through the list that follows and check those that you want to learn more about.

The job titles are arranged in clusters of related jobs, in the same groupings used in the *Occupational Outlook Handbook* and *America's Top 300 Jobs.* Major job groupings are identified in **bold** type, and any subgroupings are indicated *italic* type. Job titles within the groupings are in plain type.

As you review the job titles in this list, put a check mark by those that interest you. Then read about these jobs in the *OOH.*

OOH JOB CLUSTERS AND TITLES

Management and Business and Financial Operations Occupations

_____ Accountants and auditors

_____ Administrative services and facility managers

_____ Advertising, marketing, and public relations managers

_____ Budget analysts

_____ Claims adjusters, appraisers, examiners, and investigators

_____ Computer and information systems managers

_____ Construction managers

_____ Cost estimators

_____ Education administrators

_____ Engineering and natural sciences managers

_____ Farmers, ranchers, and agricultural managers

_____ Financial analysts and personal financial advisors

_____ Financial managers

_____ Food service managers

_____ Funeral directors

_____ Human resources, training, and labor relations managers and specialists

_____ Industrial production managers

_____ Insurance underwriters

_____ Loan counselors and officers

_____ Lodging managers

_____ Management analysts

_____ Medical and health services managers

_____ Property, real estate, and community association managers

_____ Purchasing managers, buyers, and purchasing agents

_____ Tax examiners, collectors, and revenue agents

_____ Top executives

(continues)

(continued)

Professional and Related Occupations

Architects, Surveyors, and Cartographers

_____ Architects, except landscape and naval

_____ Landscape architects

_____ Surveyors, cartographers, photogrammetrists, and surveying technicians

Drafters and Engineering Technicians

_____ Drafters

_____ Engineering technicians

Engineers

_____ Aerospace engineers

_____ Agricultural engineers

_____ Biomedical engineers

_____ Chemical engineers

_____ Civil engineers

_____ Computer hardware engineers

_____ Electrical and electronics engineers, except computer

_____ Environmental engineers

_____ Industrial engineers, including health and safety

_____ Materials engineers

_____ Mechanical engineers

_____ Mining and geological engineers, including mining safety engineers

_____ Nuclear engineers

_____ Petroleum engineers

Arts and Design

_____ Artists and related workers

_____ Designers

Entertainers and Performers, Sports, and Related Occupations

_____ Actors, producers, and directors

_____ Athletes, coaches, umpires, and related workers

_____ Dancers and choreographers

_____ Musicians, singers, and related workers

Media and Communications-Related Occupations

_____ Announcers

_____ Broadcast and sound engineering technicians and radio operators

_____ News analysts, reporters, and correspondents

_____ Photographers

_____ Public relations specialists

_____ Television, video, and motion picture camera operators and editors

_____ Writers and editors

Community and Social Services Occupations

_____ Clergy

    _____ Protestant ministers

    _____ Rabbis

    _____ Roman Catholic priests

_____ Counselors

_____ Probation officers and correctional treatment specialists

(continues)

(continued)

_____ Social and human service assistants

_____ Social workers

Computer and Mathematical Occupations

_____ Actuaries

_____ Computer programmers

_____ Computer software engineers

_____ Computer support specialists and systems administrators

_____ Mathematicians

_____ Operations research analysts

_____ Statisticians

_____ Systems analysts, computer scientists, and database administrators

Education, Training, Library, and Museum Occupations

_____ Archivists, curators, and museum technicians

_____ Instructional coordinators

_____ Library technicians

_____ Teacher assistants

_____ Teachers—adult literacy and remedial and self-enrichment education

_____ Teachers—postsecondary

_____ Teachers—preschool, kindergarten, elementary, middle, and secondary

_____ Teachers—special education

Legal

_____ Court reporters

_____ Judges, magistrates, and other judicial workers

_____ Lawyers

_____ Paralegals and legal assistants

Life Scientists

_____ Agricultural and food scientists

_____ Biological and medical scientists

_____ Conservation scientists and foresters

Physical Scientists

_____ Atmospheric scientists

_____ Chemists and materials scientists

_____ Environmental scientists and geoscientists

_____ Physicists and astronomers

_____ ### Science Technicians

Social Scientists and Related Occupations

_____ Economists and market and survey researchers

_____ Psychologists

_____ Urban and regional planners

_____ Social scientists, other

Health Diagnosing and Treating Occupations

_____ Chiropractors

_____ Dentists

_____ Dietitians and nutritionists

_____ Occupational therapists

_____ Optometrists

_____ Pharmacists

(continues)

(continued)

_____ Physical therapists

_____ Physician assistants

_____ Physicians and surgeons

_____ Podiatrists

_____ Recreational therapists

_____ Registered nurses

_____ Respiratory therapists

_____ Speech-language pathologists and audiologists

_____ Veterinarians

Health Technologists and Technicians

_____ Cardiovascular technologists and technicians

_____ Clinical laboratory technologists and technicians

_____ Dental hygienists

_____ Diagnostic medical sonographers

_____ Emergency medical technicians and paramedics

_____ Licensed practical and licensed vocational nurses

_____ Medical records and health information technicians

_____ Nuclear medicine technologists

_____ Occupational health and safety specialists and technicians

_____ Opticians, dispensing

_____ Pharmacy technicians

_____ Radiologic technologists and technicians

_____ Surgical technologists

Service Occupations

Building and Grounds Clearing and Maintenance Occupations

_____ Building cleaning workers

_____ Grounds maintenance workers

_____ Pest control workers

Food Preparation and Serving Related Occupations

_____ Chefs, cooks, and food preparation workers

_____ Food and beverage serving and related workers

Healthcare Support Occupations

_____ Dental assistants

_____ Medical assistants

_____ Medical transcriptionists

_____ Nursing, psychiatric, and home health aides

_____ Occupational therapist assistants and aides

_____ Pharmacy aides

_____ Physical therapist assistants and aides

Personal Care and Service Occupations

_____ Animal care and service workers

_____ Barbers, cosmetologists, and other personal appearance workers

_____ Childcare workers

_____ Flight attendants

_____ Gaming services occupations

_____ Personal and home care aides

_____ Recreation and fitness workers

(continues)

(continued)

Protective Service Occupations

_____ Correctional officers

_____ Firefighting occupations

_____ Police and detectives

_____ Private detectives and investigators

_____ Security guards and gaming surveillance officers

Sales and Related Occupations

_____ Cashiers

_____ Counter and rental clerks

_____ Demonstrators, product promoters, and models

_____ Insurance sales agents

_____ Real estate brokers and sales agents

_____ Retail salespersons

_____ Sales engineers

_____ Sales representatives, wholesale and manufacturing

_____ Sales worker supervisors

_____ Securities, commodities, and financial services sales agents

_____ Travel agents

Office and Administrative Support Occupations

_____ Communications equipment operators

_____ Computer operators

_____ Data entry and information processing workers

_____ Desktop publishers

Financial Clerks

_____ Bill and account collectors

_____ Billing and posting clerks and machine operators

_____ Bookkeeping, accounting, and auditing clerks

_____ Gaming cage workers

_____ Payroll and timekeeping clerks

_____ Procurement clerks

_____ Tellers

Information and Record Clerks

_____ Brokerage clerks

_____ Credit authorizers, checkers, and clerks

_____ Customer service representatives

_____ File clerks

_____ Hotel, motel, and resort desk clerks

_____ Human resources assistants, except payroll and timekeeping

_____ Interviewers

_____ Library assistants, clerical

_____ Order clerks

_____ Receptionists and information clerks

_____ Reservation and transportation ticket agents and travel clerks

Material Recording, Scheduling, Dispatching, and Distributing Occupations, Except Postal Workers

_____ Cargo and freight agents

_____ Couriers and messengers

_____ Dispatchers

_____ Meter readers, utilities

_____ Production, planning, and expediting clerks

_____ Shipping, receiving, and traffic clerks

(continues)

(continued)

_____ Stock clerks and order fillers

_____ Weighers, measurers, checkers, and samplers, recordkeeping

Other Office and Administrative Support Occupations

_____ Office and administrative support worker supervisors and managers

_____ Office clerks, general

_____ Postal Service workers

_____ Secretaries and administrative assistants

Farming, Fishing, and Forestry Occupations

_____ Agricultural workers

_____ Fishers and fishing vessel operators

_____ Forest, conservation, and logging workers

Construction Trades and Related Occupations

_____ Boilermakers

_____ Brickmasons, blockmasons, and stonemasons

_____ Carpenters

_____ Carpet, floor, and tile installers and finishers

_____ Cement masons, concrete finishers, segmental pavers, and terrazzo workers

_____ Construction and building inspectors

_____ Construction equipment operators

_____ Construction laborers

_____ Drywall installers, ceiling tile installers, and tapers

_____ Electricians

_____ Elevator installers and repairers

_____ Glaziers

_____ Hazardous materials removal workers

_____ Insulation workers

_____ Painters and paperhangers

_____ Pipelayers, plumbers, pipefitters, and steamfitters

_____ Plasterers and stucco masons

_____ Roofers

_____ Sheet metal workers

_____ Structural and reinforcing iron and metal workers

Installation, Maintenance, and Repair Occupations

Electrical and Electronic Equipment Mechanics, Installers, and Repairers

_____ Computer, automated teller, and office machine repairers

_____ Electrical and electronics installers and repairers

_____ Electronic home entertainment equipment installers and repairers

_____ Radio and telecommunications equipment installers and repairers

Vehicle and Mobile Equipment Mechanics, Installers, and Repairers

_____ Aircraft and avionics equipment mechanics and service technicians

_____ Automotive body and related repairers

_____ Automotive service technicians and mechanics

_____ Diesel service technicians and mechanics

_____ Heavy vehicle and mobile equipment service technicians and mechanics

(continues)

(continued)

_____ Small engine mechanics

Other Installation, Maintenance, and Repair Occupations

_____ Coin, vending, and amusement machine servicers and repairers

_____ Heating, air-conditioning, and refrigeration mechanics and installers

_____ Home appliance repairers

_____ Industrial machinery installation, repair, and maintenance workers

_____ Line installers and repairers

_____ Precision instrument and equipment repairers

Production Occupations

_____ Assemblers and fabricators

_____ Food processing occupations

Metal Workers and Plastic Workers

_____ Computer control programmers and operators

_____ Machinists

_____ Machine setters, operators, and tenders—metal and plastic

_____ Tool and die makers

_____ Welding, soldering, and brazing workers

Plant and System Operators

_____ Power plant operators, distributors, and dispatchers

_____ Stationary engineers and boiler operators

_____ Water and liquid waste treatment plant and system operators

Printing Occupations

_____ Bookbinders and bindery workers

_____ Prepress technicians and workers

_____ Printing machine operators

Other Production Occupations

_____ Dental laboratory technicians

_____ Inspectors, testers, sorters, samplers, and weighers

_____ Jewelers and precious stone and metal workers

_____ Ophthalmic laboratory technicians

_____ Painting and coating workers, except construction and maintenance

_____ Photographic process workers and processing machine operators

_____ Semiconductor processors

_____ Textile, apparel, and furnishings occupations

_____ Woodworkers

Transportation and Material Moving Occupations

Air Transportation Occupations

_____ Aircraft pilots and flight engineers

_____ Air traffic controllers

_____ Material moving occupations

Motor Vehicle Operators

_____ Busdrivers

_____ Taxi drivers and chauffeurs

_____ Truckdrivers and driver/sales workers

(continues)

(continued)

Other Transportation Occupations

_____ Rail transportation occupations

_____ Water transportation occupations

_____ **Job Opportunities in the Armed Forces**

Explore Specific Industries

The industry you work in can often be just as important as the occupation you select. For example, if you are interested in the medical field but are looking for a position using your accounting skills—why not consider looking for an accounting-related job in the medical industry? Some industries will simply be more interesting to you than others, so focus your job search in those industries.

Another good reason to consider various industries is that some are likely to pay more than others do, often for the same skills or jobs. So, if the industry where you apply your skills is not that important to you, why not look in an industry that tends to pay better?

The *Career Guide to Industries*, another book by the U.S. Department of Labor, contains very helpful reviews for each of the major industries mentioned in the following list. Organized in groups of related industries, this list covers about 70% of the nation's workforce.

Put a check mark by industries that interest you, and then learn more about the opportunities they present. Many libraries and bookstores carry the *Career Guide to Industries*, or you can find the information on the Internet at www.bls.gov/oco/cg/ or at www.CareerOINK.com.

MAJOR U.S. INDUSTRIES

Agriculture, Mining, and Construction

_____ Agricultural Production

_____ Agricultural Services

_____ Construction

_____ Mining and Quarrying

_____ Oil and Gas Extraction

Manufacturing

_____ Aerospace Manufacturing

_____ Apparel and Other Textile Products

_____ Chemicals Manufacturing, Except Drugs

_____ Drug Manufacturing

_____ Electronic Equipment Manufacturing

_____ Food Processing

_____ Motor Vehicle and Equipment Manufacturing

_____ Printing and Publishing

_____ Steel Manufacturing

_____ Textile Mill Products

Transportation, Communications, and Public Utilities

_____ Air Transportation

_____ Cable and Other Pay Television Services

_____ Public Utilities

_____ Radio and Television Broadcasting

_____ Telecommunications

_____ Trucking and Warehousing

Wholesale and Retail Trade

_____ Department, Clothing, and Accessory Stores

_____ Eating and Drinking Places

(continues)

(continued)

_____ Grocery Stores

_____ Motor Vehicle Dealers

_____ Wholesale Trade

Finance and Insurance

_____ Banking

_____ Insurance

_____ Securities and Commodities

Services

_____ Advertising

_____ Amusement and Recreation Services

_____ Child-Care Services

_____ Computer and Data Processing

_____ Educational Services

_____ Health Services

_____ Hotels and Other Lodging Places

_____ Management and Public Relations Services

_____ Motion Picture Production and Distribution

_____ Personnel Supply Services

_____ Social Services, Except Child Care

Government

_____ Federal Government, Excluding the Postal Service

_____ State and Local Government, Excluding Education and Hospitals

Go back over your lists of job titles and industries. For the first two items below, list the jobs that interest you most. Then select the industries that interest you most and list them in the third space.

These are the jobs and industries you should research most carefully. Your ideal job is likely to be found in some combination of these jobs and industries, or in more specialized but related jobs and industries.

The 5 Job Titles That Interest You Most

_____

_____

_____

_____

_____

The 5 Next Most Interesting Job Titles

_____

_____

_____

_____

_____

The Industries That Interest You Most

_____

_____

_____

_____

_____

And, Now, We Return to Job-Related Skills

Back on pages 18 and 19, I suggested that you should first define the job you want and then identify key job-related skills you have that support your ability to do it. These are the job-related skills to emphasize in interviews.

So, now that you have defined your ideal job, you can pinpoint the job-related skills it requires. Complete the Essential Job Search Data Worksheet in Appendix A (pages 119 to 129).

Yes, completing the Essential Job Search Data Worksheet requires time, but doing so will help you clearly define key skills to emphasize in interviews, when what you say matters so much. So look at the worksheet now, and promise to do it tonight. Really. People who complete that worksheet will do better in their interviews than those who don't.

After you complete the Essential Job Search Data Worksheet, go back to page 13 and write in Your Top Five Job-Related Skills. Include there the job-related skills you have that you would most like to use in your next job.

Use the Most Effective Methods to Get a Better Job in Less Time

Employer surveys found that most employers don't advertise their job openings. They most often hire people they already know, people who find out about the jobs through word of mouth, or people who happen to be in the right place at the right time. While luck plays a part, you can increase your "luck" in finding job openings.

Let's look at the job search methods that people use. The U.S. Department of Labor conducts a regular survey of unemployed people actively looking for work. The survey results follow.

Percentage of Unemployed Using Various Job Search Methods

- ◆ Contacted employer directly: 64.5%
- ◆ Sent out resumes/filled out applications: 48.3%
- ◆ Contacted public employment agency: 20.4%
- ◆ Placed or answered help wanted ads: 14.5%
- ◆ Contacted friends or relatives: 13.5%
- ◆ Contacted private employment agency: 6.6%
- ◆ Used other active search methods: 4.4%
- ◆ Contacted school employment center: 2.3%
- ◆ Checked union or professional registers: 1.5%

Source: U.S. Department of Labor, Current Population Survey

What Job Search Methods Work Best?

The survey shows that most people use more than one job search technique. For example, one person might read want ads, fill out applications, and ask friends for job leads. Others might send out resumes, contact everyone they know from professional contacts, and sign up at employment agencies.

But the survey covered only nine job search methods and asked only whether the job seeker did or did not use each method. The survey did not cover Internet job searches, nor did it ask whether a method actually worked in getting job offers.

Unfortunately, there hasn't been much recent research on the effectiveness of various job search methods. Most of what we know is based on older research and the observations of people who work with job seekers. I'll share what we do know about the effectiveness of job search methods in the content that follows.

Get the Most Out of Less-Effective Job Search Methods

The truth is that every job search method works for someone. But experience and research show that some methods are more effective than others are. Your task in the job search is to spend more of your time using more effective methods—and increase the effectiveness of all the methods you use.

So let's start by looking at some traditional job search methods and how you can increase their effectiveness. Only about one-third of all job seekers get their jobs using one of these methods, but you should still consider using them.

> **Quip**
>
> **Your job search objective:**
>
> Almost everyone finds a job eventually, so your objective should be to find a good job in less time. The job search methods I emphasize in this book will help you do just that.

Newspaper and Internet Help Wanted Ads

Most jobs are never advertised, and only about 15 percent of all people get their jobs through the want ads. Everyone who reads the paper knows about these openings, so competition is fierce for the few advertised jobs.

The Internet also lists many job openings. But, as happens with newspaper ads, enormous numbers of people view these postings. Some people do get jobs this way, so go ahead and apply. Just be sure to spend most of your time using more effective methods.

Internet job seeking is covered in more detail later in this step.

Filling Out Applications

Most employers require job seekers to complete an application form. Applications are designed to collect negative information, and employers use applications to screen people out. If, for example, your training or work history is not the best, you will often never get an interview, even if you can do the job.

Completing applications is a more-effective approach for young and entry-level job seekers. The reason is that there is a shortage of workers for the relatively low-paying jobs that less-experienced job seekers typically seek. As a result, when trying to fill those positions, employers are more willing to accept a lack of experience or job skills.

Even so, you will get better results by filling out the application, if asked to do so, and then requesting an interview with the person in charge.

When you complete an application, make it neat and error-free, and do not include anything that could get you screened out. If necessary, leave a problem section blank. It can always be explained after you get an interview.

Employment Agencies

There are three types of employment agencies. One is operated by the government and is free. The others are run as for-profit businesses and charge a fee to either you or an employer. Here are the advantages and disadvantages of using each.

The government employment service and one-stop centers. Each state has a network of local offices to pay unemployment compensation, provide job leads, and offer other services at no charge to you or to employers. The service's name varies by state. It may be called "Job Service," "Department of Labor," "Unemployment Office," "Workforce Development," or another name.

Many states also have "One-Stop Centers" that provide employment counseling, reference books, computerized career information, job listings, and other resources.

> ### Quip
>
> **Whatever works is good.**
>
> I am NOT suggesting that you should NEVER use less-effective techniques. Some people get very good jobs using the worst of methods, and that is fine with me. I AM suggesting that you use a VARIETY of methods, spending most of your time using techniques that work best for most people.

The Internet site www.doleta.gov/uses will give you information on the programs provided by the government employment service, plus links to other useful sites. Another Internet site, America's Job Bank at www.ajb.dni.us, allows visitors to see all jobs listed with the government employment service and to search for jobs by region and other criteria.

The government employment service lists only 5 to 10 percent of the available openings nationally, and only about 6 percent of all job seekers get their jobs there. Even so, visit your local office early in your job search. Find out if you qualify for unemployment compensation and learn more about its services. Look into it—the price is right.

Private employment agencies. Private employment agencies are businesses that charge a fee either to you or to the employer who hires you. Fees can be from less than one month's pay to 15 percent or more of your annual salary. You will often see these agencies' ads in the help wanted section of the newspaper. Many have Web sites.

Be careful about using fee-based employment agencies. Recent research indicates that more people use and benefit from fee-based agencies than in the past. However, relatively few people who register with private agencies get a job through them.

If you use a private employment agency, ask for interviews with employers who will pay the agency's fee. Do not sign an exclusive agreement or be pressured into accepting a job, and continue to actively look for your own leads. You can find these agencies in the phone book's yellow pages, and a government-run Web site at www.ajb.dni.us lists many of them as well.

Temporary agencies. Temporary agencies offer jobs lasting from several days to many months. They charge the employer a fee per hour, and then pay you a bit less and keep the difference. You pay no direct fee to the agency. Many private employment agencies now provide temporary jobs as well.

Temp agencies have grown rapidly for good reason. They provide employers with short-term help, and employers often use them to find people they may want to hire later.

School and Employment Services

Contacting a school employment center is one of the job search methods included in the survey presented earlier. Only a small percentage of respondents used this option. This is probably because few had the service available to them.

Quip

"Temp" while looking for long-term.

Temp agencies can help you survive between jobs and get experience in different work settings. Temp jobs provide a very good option while you look for long-term work, and you may get a job offer while working as a temp. Holding a temporary job may even lead to a regular job with the same or a similar employer.

If you are a student or graduate, find out about these services at your school. Some schools provide free career counseling, resume-writing help, referrals to job openings, career interest tests, reference materials, and other services.

Special career programs work with veterans, people with disabilities, welfare recipients, union members, professional groups, and many others. Check out these services and consider using them.

Mailing Resumes and Posting Them on the Internet

Many job search "experts" used to suggest that sending out lots of resumes was a great technique. That advice probably helped sell their resume books, but mailing resumes to people you do not know was never an effective approach. Every so often this would work, but a 95 percent failure rate and few interviews were the more common outcomes, and still are.

Although mailing your resume to strangers doesn't make much sense, posting it on the Internet might because

- ◆ It doesn't take much time.

- ◆ Many employers have the potential of finding your resume there.

Still, job searching on the Internet has its limitations, just like other methods do.

I do believe that most job seekers should have a good resume. How you use it to get results is the issue. I'll cover electronic resumes in more detail later and provide tips on using the Internet throughout this book.

The Two Job Search Methods That Work Best

The fact is that most jobs are not advertised. So, how do *you* find them? The same way about two-thirds of all job seekers do—networking with people you know (which I call making *warm contacts*) and directly contacting employers (which I call making *cold contacts*). Both of these methods are based on the job search rule that you should know above all:

Employers fill most jobs with people they meet before a job is formally "open." So, the trick is to meet people who can hire you before a job is formally available. Instead of asking, "Do you have any jobs open?" I suggest that you say, "I realize you may not have any openings now, but I would still like to talk to you about the possibility of future openings."

This simple change in how you approach the job search can make an enormous difference in your getting interviews while others wait for jobs to be advertised. They remain unemployed, while you get interviews and job offers. Here are some details on how to do this most effectively.

Most-Effective Job Search Method #1: Develop a Network of Contacts

One study found that 40 percent of all people located their jobs through a lead provided by a friend, a relative, or an acquaintance. That makes people you know the #1 source of job leads—asking their help is more effective than all other job search methods.

Five Easy Steps to Develop a Network of Contacts

Developing contacts is called *networking,* and here's how it works:

1. **Make lists of people you know.**

   Make a thorough list of anyone you are friendly with. Then make a separate list of all your relatives. These two lists alone often add up to 25 to 100 people or more. Next, think of other groups of people who you have something in common with, such as former coworkers or classmates, members of your social or sports groups, members of your professional association, former employers, neighbors, and other groups. You may not know many of these people personally or well, but most will help you if you ask them.

Quip

Job seeking is a contact sport.

It's true. You have to know someone to get a job. I have found, though, that you can quickly get to know all sorts of new people if you go about it right. One of them often turns out to be the someone you need.

Make a separate networking list for each group. Check any of the following groups that make sense for your situation.

_____ Friends

_____ Relatives

_____ Friends of parents

_____ Former coworkers

_____ Members of my church or religious group

_____ People who sell me things (insurance agent, real estate agent, landlord, etc.)

_____ Neighbors

_____ People I went to school with

_____ Former teachers

_____ Members of social clubs

_____ People who provide me with services (hair stylist, counselor, mechanic, etc.)

_____ Former employers

_____ Members of sports or hobby groups

_____ Members of professional organizations I belong to or can join

Write in other groups here:

_____

_____

_____

_____

Next, list names and contact information for each person in each group. It may take some research to collect all the names and contact information, so start with lists of friends and relatives, whose information is easy to get. Some lists, like those from alumni associations or professional organizations, can also be obtained with a quick phone call or e-mail, or by searching a Web site.

2. **Contact them in a systematic way.**

Contact each person on your lists. Obviously, some people will be more helpful than others are, but any one of them might help you find a job lead.

3. **Present yourself well.**

Begin with your friends and relatives. Call and tell them you are looking for a job and need their help. Be as clear as possible about the type of employment you want and the skills and qualifications you have. Look at the sample JIST Card and phone script later in this chapter for good presentation ideas.

4. **Ask contacts for leads.**

It is possible that your contacts will know of a job opening that interests you. If so, get the details and get right on it! More likely, however, they will not, so you should ask each person the Three Magic Networking Questions.

The Three Magic Networking Questions

◆ **Do you know of any openings for a person with my skills?**
If the answer is "No" (which it usually is), then ask…

◆ **Do you know of someone else who might know of such an opening?**
If your contact does, get that name and ask for another one. If he or she doesn't, ask…

◆ **Do you know of anyone who might know of someone else who might know of a job opening?**
Another good way to ask this is "Do you know someone who knows lots of people?" If all else fails, this will usually get you a name.

---

5. **Contact these referrals and ask them the same questions.**

From each person you contact, try to get two names of other people you might contact. Doing this consistently can extend your network of acquaintances by hundreds of people. Eventually, one of these people will hire you or refer you to someone who will!

If you are persistent in doing these five steps, networking may be the only job search method you need. It works.

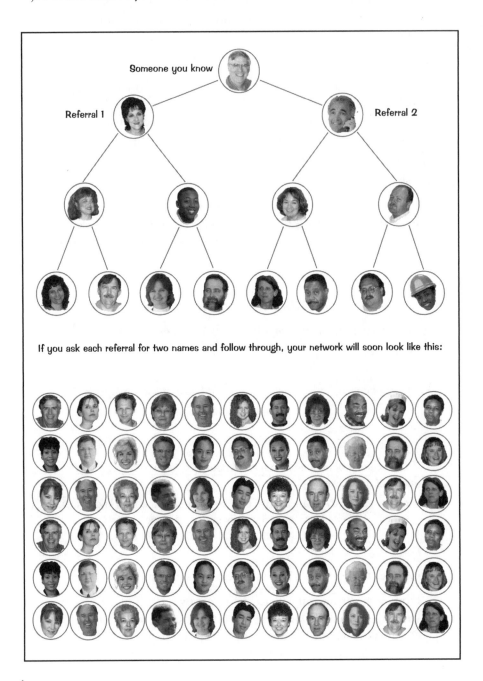

Someone you know

Referral 1

Referral 2

If you ask each referral for two names and follow through, your network will soon look like this:

Most-Effective Job Search Method #2: Contact Employers Directly

It takes more courage, but making direct contact with employers is a very effective job search technique. I call these *cold contacts* because people you don't know in advance will need to warm up to your inquiries. Two basic techniques for making cold contacts follow.

Use the Yellow Pages to Find Potential Employers

Begin by looking at the index in the front of your phone book's yellow pages. For each entry, ask yourself, "Would an organization of this kind need a person with my skills?" If you answer "Yes," then that organization or business type is a possible target. You can also rate "Yes" entries based on your interests, writing a "1" next to those that seem very interesting, a "2" next to those that you are not sure of, and a "3" next to those that aren't interesting at all.

The reason most jobs are not advertised:

Three out of four jobs are never advertised because employers don't need to advertise or want to. Employers trust people referred to them by someone they know far more than they trust someone selected from a group of unknown strangers. Most jobs are filled by referrals and people whom the employer knows. This eliminates the need to advertise. So, your job search must involve more than looking at ads.

Here is one section of a yellow pages listing that has been marked by a person looking for a position in health care.

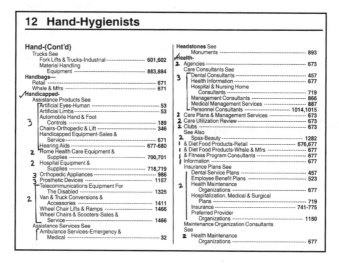

Next, select a type of organization that got a "Yes" response and turn to that section of the yellow pages. Call each organization listed there and ask to speak to the person who is most likely to hire or supervise you. This would typically be the manager of the business, or a department head—not the personnel manager.

Note: *You can easily adapt this approach to the Internet. Use sites such as www.yellowpages.com to get phone or e-mail contacts anywhere in the world.*

A Sample Phone Contact

Here is an example of a carefully scripted phone call made to the manager of a small business. You will learn more about how to create these later in this chapter.

"Hello, my name is John Kijek. I am interested in a position as an auto mechanic. I have more than three years of experience, including one year in a full-time auto mechanic's training program. I am familiar with all hand tools and electronic diagnostic equipment, and can handle common auto repair tasks, such as tune-ups, brakes, exhaust systems, and electrical and mechanical repairs. I also work quickly, often completing jobs correctly in less than the standard time. I have all the tools needed to start work immediately. I can work any shift and prefer full-time work. I am also honest, reliable, and good with people. When may I come in for an interview?"

Drop In Without an Appointment

Another effective cold contact method is to just walk into a business or organization that interests you and ask to speak to the person in charge.

> **Quip**
>
> The almost perfect source of free contacts:
>
> Your phone book's yellow pages provide the most complete and up-to-date listing of potential job search targets you can get. It even organizes them into categories that are most useful for a job seeker. Just find a category that interests you, call each listing, and ask to speak with the person who is most able to hire or supervise someone with your skills.

Remember to say that you realize there may not be a job opening now, but that you would like to be considered for a future opening. If your timing is inconvenient, ask for a better time to come back for an interview.

Try this four or five times, and you will be surprised to find that you will often get one or two interviews just this way.

Particularly effective in small businesses, dropping in also works surprisingly well in larger ones. Look for drop-in opportunities on your way to or from another interview.

It is an unconventional approach that can work very well, letting you see employers before they have an opening. And, if they like you and if you stay in touch, they are more likely to hire you than to advertise.

◆

Most Jobs Are with Small Employers

Businesses and organizations with 250 or fewer employees employ about 70 percent of all U.S. workers. They are also the source for up to 80 percent of the new jobs created each year. They are simply too important to overlook in your job search! Many of them don't have personnel departments, making direct contacts even easier and more effective.

◆

Use JIST Cards®—An Effective Mini Resume

Look at the sample cards that follow—they are JIST Cards, and they get results. Computer printed or even neatly written on 3-by-5-inch cards, JIST Cards include the essential information employers want to know.

I developed this concept years ago, and, ever since, JIST Cards have been used by thousands of job search programs and millions of people. Employers like their direct and timesaving format, and they have been proven as an effective tool to get job leads. Attach one to your resume. Give JIST Cards to friends, relatives, and other contacts and ask them to pass the cards along to others who might know of an opening. Enclose them in thank-you notes after an interview. Leave them with employers as a business card. However you get your JIST Cards into circulation, you may be surprised at how well they work.

You can easily create JIST Cards on a computer and print them on card stock you can buy at any office supply store. Or have a few hundred printed cheaply by a local quick print shop. While they are often done as 3-by-5 cards, they can be printed in any size or format. Look at the sample cards that follow for ideas on creating your own.

The Anatomy of a JIST Card

There is more to a well-written JIST Card than meets the eye. Look over the different sections of a JIST Card in the sample. Additional details on each part of a JIST Card are provided after the card.

Sample JIST Card

Sandra Zaremba

Home phone: (219) 232-7608
E-mail: SKZ1128@aol.com

Position: General Office/Clerical

Over two years' experience, plus one year of training in office practices. Familiar with a variety of computer programs, including word processing, spreadsheets, accounting, and some database and graphic design programs. Am Internet literate and word-process 70wpm accurately. Can post general ledger and handle payables, receivables, and most accounting tasks. Responsible for daily deposits averaging more than $200,000 monthly. Good interpersonal skills. Can meet strict deadlines and handle pressure well.

Willing to work any hours.

Organized, honest, reliable, and hard working.

A JIST Card is small, so it can't contain many details. A JIST Card should list only the information that is most important to employers. For a simple card, consider all that Sandra's sample includes:

◆ **Identification**

Sandra's name is given.

◆ **Two ways to make contact**

Sandra lists two ways she can be reached: a home phone number and her e-mail address. Employers want to reach you quickly, so include at least two ways you can be contacted. Because employers usually won't respond to you by letter, don't give your address. Instead, list any two of the following: a regular phone number, a cell phone number, a pager number, or an e-mail address. If you give a phone number, make sure that the phone is answered professionally by a person, voice mail, or an answering machine.

◆ **Position desired**

Sandra includes a broad job objective. This encourages an employer to consider her for many jobs.

◆ **Length of experience**

Sandra lists her total length of work experience. Some of this experience was in part-time and volunteer jobs, something she can explain in an interview.

◆ **Education and training**

Sandra lists her total time spent in training.

◆ **Job-related skills, performance, and results**

This section tells a little about what Sandra can do and how well she can do it. She describes important job-related skills for doing this work. Sandra mentions the key self-management and transferable skills she learned or used in her work and other experiences. Note that she includes several numbers. The first is "70 wpm," which means she types quickly at 70 words per minute. She states that she was responsible for $200,000 in cash deposits each month. This tells employers that she can be trusted with substantial responsibility.

◆ **Special conditions**

Sandra mentions that she is willing to work any hours. This shows that she is flexible and amenable to work.

◆ **Good worker traits and adaptive skills**

Sandra lists her key personality traits and adaptive skills that would be important to an employer. (Adaptive skills are the self-management skills explored under Step 1. They describe your basic personality and your ability to adapt to new environments.)

All this on a 3-by-5-inch card that can be read in less than 30 seconds!

Following are some more sample JIST Cards. They are for different jobs, from entry-level to those requiring more experience. Study them and use any ideas that help you write your own JIST Cards. Although you can type or even handwrite your cards, most people user a desktop computer and laser print.

Jonathan McLaughlin
Answering machine: (509) 674-8736
Cell phone: (509) 541-0981

Objective: Electronics—Installation, maintenance, and sales

Skills: Four years of work experience, plus two years' advanced training in electronics. AS degree in Electronics Engineering Technology. Managed a $500,000/year business while going to school full time, with grades in the top 25%. Familiar with all major electronics diagnostic and repair equipment. Hands-on experience with medical, consumer, communications, business, and industrial electronics equipment and applications. Good problem-solving and communications skills. Customer service oriented.

Willing to do what it takes to get the job done.

Self-motivated, dependable, learn quickly.

Jonathan is a new graduate from a two-year technical program. He was always interested in electronics, but worked in construction jobs after high school. He then got a job helping the owner of a TV and electronics repair shop. He answered phones, kept the place clean, and handled other simple tasks. But, he also volunteered to fix items, and the owner started to show him how to do more complex repairs and encouraged him to go back to school.

Jonathan worked at the electronics shop for three years, scheduling his work time around school. Using this JIST Card, he eventually landed a job with a circuit board design and manufacturing company, and now earns about three times more than he did previously.

Andrea Scott   Answering machine: (639) 298-9704
                    E-mail: andys@hotmail.com

Position Desired: Warehouse Management

Skills: Three years' experience plus two years of formal business coursework. Have supervised a staff as large as eight people and warehousing operations valued at more than $4,000,000. Automated inventory operations resulting in an estimated annual savings of more than $25,000. Working knowledge of accounting, computer systems, and advanced inventory management systems.

Will work any hours.

Responsible and hard working. Can solve problems.

Andrea got her work experience in the military, where she was responsible for warehouse operations for an infantry unit. Her business education includes high school courses, military training, and some college-level course she took while in the military. It was enough for her to land a job with Federal Express, where she now supervises 14 workers.

Jafar Browning

Home: (846) 299-3643
Pager: (846) 517-4525   E-mail: JMB092@aol.com

Objective: Sales or businesslike position requiring skills in problem solving, planning, organizing, and customer service.

Skills: Two years' experience, including coursework in business, sales methods, customer service, and business software. Promoted and received several bonuses for performance. Set record for largest single sale, which exceeded $130,000. Consistent record of getting results. Excellent communications skills. Familiar with database, word processing, and spreadsheet programs. Internet literate. Enjoy challenges and accept responsibility.

Willing to relocate.

Results oriented and energetic. Good problem-solving skills.

Jafar does not have formal education beyond high school but is smart and very good with people. He used these adaptive and transferable skills in sales, where he could earn good pay. He landed a position selling telecommunications services to businesses and doubled his earnings.

John Harold
Home: (619) 433-0040   E-mail: johnharold@earthlink.net

Objective: Responsible business-management position

Skills: More than 7 years of management experience, plus a degree in Business. Managed budgets as large as $5 million. Experienced in cost control and reduction, cutting more than 20% of overheads, while sales increased almost 30%. Good organizer and problem-solver. Excellent communications skills.

Prefer responsible position in a medium-to-large business.

Cope well with deadline pressure, seek challenge, flexible.

John has lots of experience and great credentials. He accepted a job running a small window manufacturing company that is now growing rapidly.

THE JIST CARD WORKSHEET

A JIST Card is small, so it should list only the information that is most important to employers. This worksheet will help you compose your own JIST Card later. It provides tips for each section of the card. Complete each portion of the worksheet as well as you can.

Your name: _____

Tips

Keep this simple and professional. Don't use nicknames, middle names, or initials.

Contact information: _____

_____

_____

_____

Include two or more ways for an employer to contact you. Include a telephone number that will be answered all the time. Always include your area code.

If you use an answering machine or voice mail, make sure it does not have a silly greeting. If the phone is at home, make sure anyone who might answer it knows how to take accurate messages.

Include a cell phone or pager number if you have one. Including an e-mail address helps communicate that you are Internet literate.

Job objective: _____

_____

_____

_____

_____

Tips

Don't be too narrow in your job objective. Say "General office" rather than "Receptionist" if you would consider a variety of office jobs. If you are narrower in your job objective, try to avoid a narrow job title and give other details. For example, say "Management position in an insurance-related business" or "Working with children in a medical or educational setting."

Don't limit yourself to entry-level jobs if you have potential or interest in doing more. If you say "Office manager" instead of "Secretary," you just might get a more-responsible and higher-paying job. If you are not too sure of your ability to get a higher-paying job, it is still best to keep your options open. Say "Office manager or responsible secretarial position," for example.

(continues)

(continued)

Your Work Experience Statement

You should take advantage of all the experience you have that supports your job objective. Depending on your situation, you can include any or all of the following as part of your work experience:

◆ **Paid work**

List any work you were paid to do. The work does not have to be similar to the job you are looking for now. Baby-sitting and lawn-mowing jobs count. So can working in a fast-food place. If you worked part-time, estimate the total number of hours you worked. Divide this total by 160 hours to get the number of months you worked. Of course, paid work that is directly related to your job objective is the best, if you have it.

◆ **Volunteer work**

You can include volunteer work as part of your total work experience. It counts, so list it if you don't have much paid work experience.

◆ **Informal work**

Include work you did at home or as an unpaid hobby. It is best if this work relates to the job, but it doesn't have to. For example, if you worked on cars at home and want to be an auto mechanic, there is an obvious connection. You may have experience taking care of younger brothers or sisters, or working in the family business. This is real experience and, if it can help you, mention it.

◆ **Related education and training**

If you took high school or college courses that relate to the job you want, you can count this as part of your total experience. You can also count any courses or training you received in the military, business or technical school, or anywhere else. If they relate in some way to the job you want, they count.

Your Total Work Experience

Now, fill in the lines that follow. Write either years or months (if you don't have much experience) in the spaces beside each entry.

a. Total time paid work experience _____

b. Total time volunteer work   + _____

c. Total time informal work   +

d. Total time related education or
    training   + _____

    Total experience   = _____

Here are some tips for writing your experience statement.

◆ **If you have lots of work experience…**

Emphasize the closest to your job objective, if you have lots of experience. For example, if you have 20 years of total experience, include just the experience that directly relates to this job. And, say "More than 15 years of experience." This keeps the employer from knowing how old you are. Your age is an advantage you will present in the interview!

◆ **If you don't have much paid work experience…**

If you have no paid work experience related to the job you now seek, emphasize your education, training, and other work. For example, "Nearly two years of experience, including one year of advanced training in office procedures." Remember to include the total of all paid and unpaid work as part of your experience! Include all those part-time jobs and volunteer jobs by writing "More than 18 months' total work experience."

◆ **If your experience is in another field…**

Mention that you have "Four years' work experience" without saying in what field.

(continues)

(continued)

◆ **Other points to emphasize**

If you won promotions, raises, or have other special strengths, this is the time to say so. For example: "More than seven years of increasingly responsible work experience, including three years as a supervisor. Promoted twice."

Look over the sample JIST Cards for additional ideas, and then write your own statement below.

_____

_____

_____

_____

_____

Your Education and Training Statement

If it helps, you can combine your education and training with your experience on your JIST Card. Or you can list your education and training as a separate statement. Don't mention your education or training if it doesn't help you.

If you have a license, certification, or degree that supports your job objective, mention it here. For example, "Four years of experience plus two years of training leading to certification as an Emergency Medical Technician." If you want, you can revise your previous experience statement here to include your education and training.

_____

_____

_____

_____

_____

Your Key Skills Statement

List the things you can do to support your job objective. If appropriate, mention job-related tools or equipment you can use. Use the language of the job to describe the more important things you can do. Use some numbers to strengthen what you say and to emphasize results. For example, instead of writing "Can do word processing," say "Accurately word-process 80 words per minute and am familiar with advanced graphic and formatting capabilities of Microsoft Word and PageMaker."

Emphasize results! It is too easy to overlook the importance of what you do. Add up the number of transactions you handled, the money you were responsible for, the results you got. For example, a person with fast-food experience might write, "Have handled more than 50,000 customer contacts quickly and accurately with total sales of over $250,000." These numbers are based on a five-day workweek, 200 customers a day for one year, and an average sale of $5.

Impressive numbers, when presented in this way. The fact that this was done in a fast-food job does not have to be mentioned. These "lowly" jobs often require hard work, speed, and advanced skills that can be promoted to employers. Someone who ran a small store could say, "Responsible for business with more than $150,000 in sales per year. Increased sales by 35% within 18 months." Someone with reception, customer service, or sales experience might note her "Good appearance and pleasant telephone voice."

It is certainly OK to give numbers to support these skills, too. Think hard about your experiences and try to include numbers and results. Look over the sample JIST Cards for ideas, and then write your own statement below. _____

_____

_____

_____

_____

_____

(continues)

Special Conditions or Preferred Working Conditions Statement

This is an optional section in which you can add just a few words to let the employer know what you are willing to do. Do not limit your employment possibilities by saying "Will only work days" or "No travel wanted." Look at the sample JIST Cards for ideas, and then write your own statement below.

_____

_____

_____

Your Good Worker Traits and Skills Statement

Refer to Step 1, then list three or four of your key adaptive (self-management) skills below. Choose skills that are most important in the job you are seeking.

_____

_____

_____

_____

Now Write and Use Your JIST Card

You will have to revise the content from the worksheet you just completed so that all your information fits onto a 3-by-5-inch card. To do so, make every word count. Get rid of anything that does not directly support your job objective. Use short phrases; you don't have to use complete sentences. Add more information if your JIST Card is too short, but add things only if they make your statements stronger. Get rid of anything that does not present you in a positive way.

Hand-write or print your content on a 3-by-5 card to help you see if you have included too much or too little information. Edit it again as needed to make it fit. Reading your JIST Card out loud will help you to know how it sounds and may give you additional ideas to improve it. Ask someone else to help you with the final version so that it has no grammar or spelling errors.

Once you have your final content, you'll want to put lots of your JIST Cards in circulation. While you can type or even hand-write individual JIST Cards, it is best to have them printed in quantities of at least 100 to 500. You can print your own JIST Cards on a computer or have them done at most print shops for a modest fee.

You can fit five copies of a JIST Card on one standard sheet of 8½-by-11-inch light card stock (available at most office supply stores and printers). You will need to cut the sheets down to the correct size of the individual cards. Office supply stores may also sell "micro-perforated" sheets that easily can be torn into 3-by-5-inch cards. This lets you produce the cards on your own printer without having to divide the sheets yourself.

Use Your JIST Card as the Basis for an Effective Phone Script

Once you have created your JIST Card, you can use it as the basis for a phone "script" to make warm or cold calls. Revise your JIST Card content so that it sounds natural when spoken, and then edit it until you can read it out loud in about 30 seconds. The sample phone script that follows is based on the content of a JIST Card. Use it to help you modify your own JIST Card into a phone script.

> *"Hello, my name is Pam Nykanen. I am interested in a position in hotel management. I have four years' experience in sales, catering, and accounting with a 300-room hotel. I also have an associate degree in hotel management, plus one year of experience with the Bradey Culinary Institute. During my employment, I helped double revenues from meetings and conferences and increased bar revenues by 46 percent. I have good problem-solving skills and am good with people. I am also well organized, hard working, and detail oriented. When may I come in for an interview?"*

Once you have your script, make some practice calls to warm or cold contacts. If making cold calls, contact the person most likely to supervise you. Then present your script just as you practiced it, without stopping.

Making cold calls takes guts, but job search programs find that most people can get one or more interviews an hour using cold calls. Start by calling people you know and the people they refer you to. Then try calls to businesses that don't sound very interesting. As you get better, call more desirable targets. Hey, what's the worst that could happen?

While the sample script assumes that you are calling someone you don't know, it can be changed to address warm contacts and referrals. Making cold calls takes courage—but works very well for many who are willing to do it.

Tips for Using the Internet in Your Job Search

I provide Internet-related tips throughout this book, but it deserves a separate section, so here it is.

The Internet has limitations as a job search tool. While many have used it to get job leads, it has not worked well for far more. Too many assume they can simply add their resume to resume databases, and employers will line up to hire them. Just as with the older approach of sending out lots of resumes, good things sometimes happen, but not often.

Quip

Dialing for dollars:

The phone is an essential job search tool that can get you more interviews per hour than any other job search tool. But it won't work unless you use it actively throughout your job search!

I recommend two points of view that apply to all job search methods, including the Internet:

REMEMBER...
IT IS UNWISE TO RELY ON JUST ONE OR TWO METHODS IN CONDUCTING YOUR JOB SEARCH.
IT IS ESSENTIAL THAT YOU USE AN ACTIVE RATHER THAN A PASSIVE APPROACH IN YOUR JOB SEARCH.

Ways to Increase Your Internet Effectiveness

I encourage you to use the Internet in your job search but suggest that you use it along with other techniques, including direct contacts with employers. The following suggestions can increase the effectiveness of using the Internet in your job search:

◆ **Be as specific as possible in identifying the job you seek.**

This is important in using any job search method and even more so in looking for jobs on the Internet. The Internet is enormous, so it is essential to be as focused as possible in what you are searching for. Narrow your job title or titles to be as specific as possible. Limit your search to specific industries or areas of specialization.

◆ **Have reasonable expectations.**

Success on the Internet is more likely if you understand its limitations. For example, employers trying to find someone with skills in high demand, such as network engineers or nurses, are more likely to use the Internet to recruit job candidates.

◆ **Limit your geographic options.**

If you don't want to move, or would move but only to certain areas, state this preference on your resume and restrict your search to those areas. Many Internet sites allow you to view only those jobs that meet your location criteria.

◆ **Create an electronic resume.**

With few exceptions, resumes submitted on the Internet end up as simple text files with no graphic elements. Employers search databases of many resumes for those that include key words or meet other searchable criteria. So create a simple text resume for Internet use and include on it words likely to be used by employers searching for someone with your abilities.

- **Get your resume into the major resume databases.**

  Most Internet employment sites let you add your resume for free, and then charge employers to advertise openings or to search for candidates. These easy-to-use sites often provide all sorts of useful information for job seekers.

- **Make direct contacts.**

  Visit Web sites of organizations that interest you and learn more about them. Some will post openings, allow you to apply online, or even provide access to staff who can answer your questions. Even if they don't, you can always e-mail a request for the name of the person in charge of the work that interests you and then communicate with that person directly.

- **Network.**

  You can network online, too, finding names and e-mail addresses of potential employer contacts or of other people who might know someone with job openings. Look at interest groups, professional association sites, alumni sites, chat rooms, and employer sites—these are just some of the many creative ways to network and interact with people via the Internet.

Useful Internet Sites

Thousands of Internet sites provide information on careers or education. Many have links to other sites that they recommend. Service providers such as America Online (www.aol.com) and the Microsoft Network (www.msn.com) have career information and job listings, plus links to other sites. Larger portal sites offer links to recommended career-related sites. Alta Vista (www.altavista.com), Lycos (www.lycos.com), and Yahoo! (www.yahoo.com) are just a few of these portals.

These major career-specific sites can get you started:

- The Riley Guide
  www.rileyguide.com

- America's Job Bank
  www.ajb.dni.us

- The JIST site
  www.jist.com

- CareerPath.com
  www.careerpath.com

- Monster.com
  www.monster.com

CareerOINK.com provides career information and links to other sites.

Write a Simple Resume Now and a Better One Later

You've already learned that sending out paper resumes and waiting for responses is passive and not an effective job-seeking technique. Posting your resume on one or more Internet sites is also passive but can make sense if you use more active approaches, too.

The fact is that many employers *will* ask you for a paper or Internet resume, so a resume can be a useful tool in your job search. Unfortunately, too many people spend weeks working on their resume when they should be out getting interviews instead.

So I suggest you begin with a simple resume you can complete quickly and start using today. If you want a "better" resume, you can work on it on weekends and evenings.

Tips for Creating a Superior Resume

The following are some basic tips that make sense for any resume format, paper or electronic.

Write It Yourself

It's okay to look at other resumes for ideas, but write yours yourself. It will force you to organize your thoughts and background.

Make It Error-Free

One spelling or grammar error will create a negative impressionist (see what I mean?). Get someone else to review your final draft for any errors. Then review it again because these rascals have a way of slipping in.

Make It Look Good

Poor copy quality, cheap paper, bad type quality, or anything else that creates a poor appearance will turn off employers to even the best resume content. Internet resumes have format rules of their own, and you will need to make them look presentable in that format.

Get professional help with design and printing, if necessary. Many professional resume writers and even print shops offer writing and desktop design services.

Be Brief; Be Relevant

Many good resumes fit on one page, and few justify more than two. Include only the most important points. Use short sentences and action words.

If it doesn't relate to and support the job objective, cut it!

Be Honest

Don't overstate your qualifications. If you end up getting a job you can't handle, who does it help? And a lie can result in your being fired later.

Be Positive

Emphasize your accomplishments and results. A resume is no place to be too humble or to display your faults.

Be Specific

Instead of saying "I am good with people," you can say, "I supervised four people in the warehouse and increased productivity by 30 percent." Use numbers whenever possible, such as the number of people served, the dollars saved, or the percentage by which sales increased.

You should also know that everyone feels that he or she is a resume expert. Whatever you do, someone will tell you that it's wrong.

Quip

Avoid the resume pile.

Resume experts often suggest that a "dynamite" resume will jump out of the pile. This is old-fashioned advice. It assumes that you are applying to large organizations and for advertised jobs. Today, most jobs are with small employers and are not advertised. My advice is to avoid joining that stack of resumes in the first place, by looking for openings that others overlook.

Remember that a resume is simply a job search tool. You should never delay or slow down your job search because your resume is not "good enough." The best approach is to create a simple and acceptable resume as quickly as possible and then use it. As time permits, create a better one if you feel you must.

The Five Most Effective Ways to Use a Resume

Even an excellent resume won't get you talking with an employer unless you use it effectively. These tips suggest how to use your resume to get more interviews:

1. **Get the interview first.**

   It is always better to contact employers by phone, e-mail, or in person *before* you send a resume. If possible, get a referral from someone you know. Or, make a cold contact directly with the employer. In either case, ask for an interview. If no opening is available now, ask whether you can come in and discuss the possibility of future openings.

2. **Then, send your resume.**

   Whenever possible, send or e-mail your resume after you schedule an interview, so that the employer can read about you before your meeting. Valuable interview time can then be spent discussing your skills rather than details that are best presented in a resume.

3. **Follow up with a JIST Card and thank-you note.**

   Immediately after an interview, send a thank-you note. Even if you use e-mail to communicate with employers, most appreciate a mailed thank-you note. And mailing the note allows you to enclose your JIST Card or another copy of your resume.

4. **Send your resume and JIST Card to everyone in your growing job search network.**

   This is an excellent way for people in your network to help you find unadvertised leads. They can pass or e-mail information to others who might be interested in a person with your skills.

5. **Send your resume in the traditional way if you can't make direct contact.**

In some situations, you can't easily make contact with an employer. This is true, for example, if you want to post your resume on the Internet. Another example is when responding to a want ad that gives only a box number. Go ahead and do these things; just plan on using more active job search methods, too.

Chronological Resumes

Most resumes use a chronological format in which the most recent experience is listed first, followed by each previous job. This arrangement works fine for someone with work experience in several similar jobs, but not as well for those with limited experience or for career changers.

Look at the following two resumes for Judith Jones. Both use the chronological approach. The first resume would work fine for most job search needs—and it could be completed in about an hour. Notice that the second one includes some improvements. The first resume is good, but most employers would like the additional positive information in the improved resume.

Tips for Writing a Simple Chronological Resume

Follow these tips for writing a basic chronological resume.

Name

Use your formal name rather than a nickname if the formal name sounds more professional—for example, Judith Jones, rather than Judy Jones.

Address and Contact Information

Avoid abbreviations in your address and include your ZIP code. If you may move soon, use a friend's address or include a forwarding address.

Most employers will not write to you, so you must provide reliable phone numbers, e-mail addresses, or other contact options. Always include your area code in your phone number because you never know where your resume might travel. If you don't have an answering machine, get one—and leave it on whenever you leave home. Make sure your voice message presents you in a professional way.

Include alternative ways to reach you, like through a cell phone or pager number and an e-mail address.

Basic Chronological Resume

Judith J. Jones

115 South Hawthorne Avenue
Chicago, Illinois 66204
(312) 653-9217 (home)
email: jj@earthlink.com

Leaves lots of options open by not using one job title.

JOB OBJECTIVE

Desire a position in the office management, accounting, or administrative assistant area. Prefer a position requiring responsibility and a variety of tasks.

EDUCATION AND TRAINING

Acme Business College, Lincoln, Illinois
Graduate of a one-year business program.

U.S. Army
Financial procedures, accounting functions.

John Adams High School, South Bend, Indiana
Diploma, business education.

Other: Continuing education classes and workshops in business communication, computer spreadsheet and database programs, scheduling systems, and customer relations.

Emphasis on all __related__ education is important, because it helps overcome her lack of "work" experience.

Everything supports her job objective

EXPERIENCE

2001-present—Claims Processor, Blue Spear Insurance Co., Wilmette, Illinois. Handle customer medical claims, develop management reports based on spreadsheets I created, exceed productivity goals.

2000-2001—Returned to school to upgrade my business and computer skills. Took courses in advanced accounting, spreadsheet and database programs, office management, human relations, and new office techniques.

1998-2000—E4, U.S. Army. Assigned to various stations as a specialist in finance operations. Promoted prior to honorable discharge.

1996-1998—Sandy's Boutique, Wilmette, Illinois. Responsible for counter sales, display design, cash register and other tasks.

1994-1996—Held part-time and summer jobs throughout high school.

Uses her education in this section to add credentials

PERSONAL

I am reliable, hard working, and good with people.

Job Objective

You should almost always have a job objective, even if it is general.

In the sample resumes, notice how Judith kept her options open with her broad job objective. Writing "secretary" or "clerical" might keep her from being considered for other jobs she might accept.

Education and Training

Include any training or education you've had that supports your job objective. If you did not finish a formal degree or program, list what you did complete and emphasize accomplishments. If your experience is not strong, include details that do support your job objective, such as related courses and extracurricular activities.

In the two examples, Judith put her business schooling in both the Education and Experience sections. Doing this filled a job gap and allowed her to present her training as equal to work experience.

Previous Experience

Include the basics such as employer name, job title, dates employed, and responsibilities. Emphasize things such as specific skills, results, accomplishments, and superior performance.

Personal Data

Do not include irrelevant details like height, weight, and marital status—doing so is considered very old-fashioned. But you can include information like hobbies or leisure activities in a special section that directly supports your job objective.

Judith Jones's basic resume includes a Personal section, in which she listed some of her strengths, traits that often aren't mentioned in a resume.

References

You do not need to list references. Employers will ask for references if they want them. If your references are particularly good, you can mention this somewhere—the last section of your resume is often a good place.

List your references on a separate page and give it to employers who ask. Ask your references what they will say about you and, if it is positive, ask them to write a letter of recommendation that you can give to employers.

Improved Chronological Resume

Judith J. Jones

115 South Hawthorne Avenue • Chicago, Illinois 66204
(312) 653-9217 (home)
email: jj@earthlink.com

Adds lots of details to reinforce skills throughout.

More details here.

JOB OBJECTIVE

Seeking position requiring excellent business management skills in an office environment. Position should require a variety of tasks, including office management, word processing, and spreadsheet and database program use.

EDUCATION AND TRAINING

Acme Business College, Lincoln, Illinois.
Completed one-year program in Professional Office Management. Grades in top 30 percent of my class. Courses included word processing, accounting theory and systems, advanced spreadsheet and database programs, time management, and basic supervision.

John Adams High School, South Bend, Indiana.
Graduated with emphasis on business courses. Excellent grades in all business topics and won top award for word-processing speed and accuracy.

Other: Continuing education programs at my own expense, including business communications, customer relations, computer applications, sales techniques, and others.

Uses numbers to reinforce results.

EXPERIENCE

2001-present—Claims Processor, Blue Spear Insurance Company, Wilmette, Illinois. Handle 50 complex medical insurance claims per day, almost 20 percent above department average. Created a spreadsheet report process that decreased department labor costs by over $30,000 a year (one position). Received two merit raises for performance.

2000-2001—Returned to business school to gain advanced skills in accounting, office management, sales and human resources. Computer courses included word processing and graphics design, accounting and spreadsheet software, and database and networking applications. Grades in top 30 percent of class.

1998-2000—Finance Specialist (E4), U.S. Army. Responsible for the systematic processing of over 200 invoices per day from commercial vendors. Trained and supervised eight employees. Devised internal system allowing 15 percent increase in invoices processed with a decrease in personnel. Managed department with a budget equivalent of over $350,000 a year. Honorable discharge.

1996-1998—Sales Associate promoted to Assistant Manager, Sandy's Boutique, Wilmette, Illinois. Made direct sales and supervised four employees. Managed daily cash balances and deposits, made purchasing and inventory decisions, and handled all management functions during owner's absence. Sales increased 26 percent and profits doubled during my tenure.

1994-1996—Held various part-time and summer jobs through high school while maintaining good grades. Earned enough to pay all personal expenses, including car and car insurance. Learned to deal with customers, meet deadlines, work hard, handle multiple priorities, and develop other skills.

SPECIAL SKILLS AND ABILITIES

Quickly learn new computer applications and am experienced with a number of business software applications. Have excellent interpersonal, written, and oral communication and math skills. Accept supervision well, am able to supervise others, and work well as a team member. Like to get things done and have an excellent attendance record.

Tips for an Improved Chronological Resume

Once you have a simple, errorless, and eye-pleasing resume, get on with your job search. There is no reason to delay! If you want to create a better resume in your spare time (evenings or weekends), try these additional tips.

Job Objective

A poorly written job objective can limit the jobs that an employer might consider you for. Think of the skills you have and the types of jobs you want to do; describe them in general terms. Instead of using a narrow job title such as "Restaurant manager," you might write "Manage a small to mid-sized business."

Education and Training

New graduates should emphasize their recent training and education more than those with a few years of related work experience would. A more detailed description of education and training might mention specific courses you took, and activities or accomplishments that support your job objective or reinforce your key skills.

Include other details that reflect how hard you work, such as working your way through school or handling family responsibilities.

Skills and Accomplishments

Include things that support your ability to do well in the job you seek now. Even small things count. Maybe your attendance was perfect, you met a tight deadline, or you did the work of others during vacations. Be specific and include numbers—even if you have to estimate them.

The improved chronological resume example features a Special Skills and Abilities section and more accomplishments and skills. Notice how numbers can reinforce results.

Job Titles

Past job titles may not accurately reflect what you did. For example, your job title may have been "Cashier," but you also opened the store, trained new staff, and covered for the boss on vacations. Perhaps "Head cashier and assistant manager" would be more accurate.

Check with your previous employer if you are not sure.

Promotions

If you were promoted or received good evaluations, say so—"Cashier, promoted to assistant manager," for example. A promotion to a more responsible job can be handled as a separate job, if doing so results in a stronger resume.

Gaps in Employment and Other Problem Areas

Employee turnover is expensive, so few employers want to hire people who won't stay or work out. Gaps in employment, jobs held for short periods, or a lack of direction in the jobs you've held are all things that concern employers.

So consider your situation and try to give an explanation of a problem area. Here are a few examples:

2001—Continued my education at...

2002—Traveled extensively throughout the United States.

2001 to present—Self-employed barn painter and widget maker.

2001—Had first child, took year off before returning to work.

Date your employment using entire years to avoid displaying an employment gap you can't explain easily. For example "2001 to 2002" can cover a few months of unemployment at the beginning of 2001.

Skills and Combination Resumes

The functional, or "skills," resume emphasizes your most important skills, supported by specific examples of how you have used them. This approach allows you to use any part of your life history to support your ability to do the job you want.

While a skills resume can be very effective, creating one requires some work. And some employers don't like skills resumes because they can hide a job seeker's faults (such as job gaps, lack of formal education, or little related work experience) better than a chronological resume. Still, a skills resume may make sense for you.

Look over the sample resume that follow for ideas. Notice it includes elements of a skills *and* a chronological resume. This so-called "combination" resume makes sense if your previous job history or education and training are positive. More combination examples follow at the end of this chapter.

Resume Design and Production Tips

What you say in your resume is very important. How you present it is just as important. Here are some brief tips that will help you create a superior resume after the writing is done.

Skip the negatives.

Remember that a resume can get you screened out, but it is up to you to get the interview and the job. So, cut out anything negative in your resume!

Make Your Resume Look Good

Make sure that your resume looks good. Word-processing software and laser printers allow you to create a professional-looking resume. All major word processors have resume-writing templates and "wizards" that make designing your resume simple.

If you are not experienced in using word-processing software, composing your resume is not the time to learn. Trust me on this.

If you don't have access to a computer and a high-quality printer, most small print shops and resume-writing services can produce a professional-looking resume for a modest cost. Unless you get their help in writing your resume, these shops should charge no more than $50 to format a one- or two-page resume.

Get Lots of Copies

Earlier in this book, you learned how you can develop hundreds of job leads through networking and cold contacts. It is to your advantage to give each contact one or more copies of your resume. Plan on having lots of copies available. You may go through several hundred before you land your job.

If you have access to a computer and a good laser printer, you can print excellent quality copies. If you don't have regular access to a computer system, you can get good photocopies made at most quick-print shops. Look in the yellow pages for listings.

Use Good Paper and Matching Envelopes

Most office supply stores and print shops have good-quality papers and matching envelopes for resumes and cover letters. The best papers have a rich look and texture. They cost more but are worth every penny. Ivory, white, and off-white are conservative colors that look professional.

Electronic and Scannable Resumes

A traditional resume is printed on paper. The Internet and other technology now often require resumes to be in electronic form.

If you plan to use the Internet in your job search, you will need to submit your resume in electronic form. Once you do so, your resume is entered into a database that might be searched by many employers.

Even if you don't plan on using the Internet, you need to understand how electronic resumes work. More and more employers are scanning the resumes they receive.

Scanners are machines that convert your resume into electronic text. This allows employers to use a computer to quickly search hundreds or thousands of resumes to find qualified applicants. The computers look for key words in the resumes—usually qualifications and skills that match the criteria needed for the open positions—and sort out the resumes with the most "hits."

Many larger employers use scanning technology. Your paper resume is likely to be scanned into a database without your knowing it.

Because electronic resumes are used differently than those on paper, it is important to understand how you can increase their effectiveness and their "readability" by a machine.

An Electronic Resume Should Have Lots of Key Words

Employers using electronic databases search for key words in resumes. So, the more key words you include, the more likely your resume will be selected. Key words are words and phrases specific to the job you want. Here are some ways to find and present key words on your resume:

♦ **Add a key word section.**

A simple technique is to add a section to your resume titled "Key Skills." You can then add key words not included elsewhere in your resume.

Combination Resume

This sample for a recent college graduate emphasizes applicable education and skills as real experience and relates all sections back to the applicant's job objective. Key adaptive and transferable skills are highlighted throughout.

A two-page combination format for a soon-to-graduate student.

Emphasizes what he can do and not just what he wants!

Jonathan McLaughlin

6926 Mapleton Court (602) 298-9704 cell phone

Phoenix, AZ 85009 jafar@quickwit.com e-mail

JOB OBJECTIVE

Position in the electronics industry requiring skills in the design, sale, installation, maintenance, or repair of computer, audio, video, and other advanced electronics. Prefer tasks needing creative problem-solving skills and customer contact.

EDUCATION

PHOENIX TECHNICAL INSTITUTE
Phoenix, AZ, Graduating in June with AS Degree in Electronics Engineering Technology, top 25% of class.

Completing a comprehensive, two-year curriculum, including over 1,000 hours of classroom instruction and advanced laboratory experience. Theoretical, practical, and hands-on knowledge of audio and RF amplifiers, AM/FM transmitter-receiver circuits, circuit board theory and practice, PC and network systems and maintenance, microwave and radar communications, digital circuits, and much more. Excellent attendance while working two jobs to pay tuition.

These statements show he is responsible, hard working, motivated.

PLAINS JUNIOR COLLEGE
Phoenix, AZ

Courses included digital electronics, programming, computer software applications, and business topics. Worked full time and maintained a B+ average.

DESERT VIEW HIGH SCHOOL
College prep courses, including advanced math, business, marketing, merchandising, computer software applications, and computer programming. Very active in varsity sports and National Honor Society for two years.

Gives lots of emphasis to recent and past education, including specific things he learned that relate to his job objective.

This section allows him to emphasize the skills from school, work, and life that support his job objective.

SKILLS

PROBLEM-SOLVING: Familiar with the underlying theory of most electronic systems and am particularly good at isolating problems by using logic and persistence. I enjoy the challenge of solving complex problems and will work long hours, if necessary, to meet a deadline.

Explains important adaptive skills

INTERPERSONAL: Have supervised five staff and trained many more. Comfortable with one-to-one and small group communications. Can explain technical issues simply to staff and customers of varying levels of sophistication. Had over 10,000 customer contacts and several written commendations.

TECHNICAL: Background in a variety of technical areas, including medical equipment, consumer electronics, computers, automated cash registers, photocopiers, and standard office and computer equipment and peripherals. Have designed special applications using sequential logic circuits and TTL logic. Constructed a microprocessor and wrote several machine language programs for this system. Can diagnose and repair problems in digital and analog circuits.

ORGANIZATIONAL: Have set up and run my own small business and worked in another responsible job while going to school full-time. Earned enough money to live independently and pay all school expenses during this time. I can work with minimal supervision and have learned to use my time efficiently.

While 2 of his 3 jobs are not related to his current objective, he uses them to support skills that will help him do his next job.

EXPERIENCE

BANDLER'S INN: 2000–present. Waiter, promoted to night manager. Complete responsibility for all operations of a shift grossing over $500,000 in sales per year. Supervised five full-time and three part-time staff. Business increased during my employment by 35% and profits by 42%, much of it due to word-of-mouth advertising of satisfied customers. *Uses numbers to reinforce his skills.*

FRANKLIN HOSPITAL: 1999-present. Electronic Service Technician Assistant. Work in General Medicine, Diagnostic Labs, and radiology departments. Assisted technicians in routine service and maintenance of a variety of hospital equipment. Left to attend school full time but continue to work weekends while attending school.

JON'S YARD SERVICE: 1998-1999. Set up a small business while in school. Worked part time and summers doing yard work. Made enough money to buy a car and save for tuition.

More examples of his willingness to work hard and meet goals.

- **Include all your important skill words.**

  If you completed the worksheets in Steps 1 and 2, include the key skills documented there.

- **Think like a prospective employer.**

  List the jobs you want. Then think of the key words employers are likely to use when searching a database.

- **Review job descriptions.**

  Carefully review descriptions for jobs you seek in major print references like the *Occupational Outlook Handbook* and the *O*NET Dictionary of Occupational Titles.* Most large Web sites that list job openings have lots of employer job postings and job descriptions to review. Corporate Web sites often post information on job openings, another source of key words. Make a list of key words in descriptions of interest and include them in your resume.

- **Be specific.**

  List certifications and licenses, name any software and machines you can operate, and include special language and abbreviations used in your field.

> ### Quip
>
> A resume is not the most effective tool for getting interviews.
>
> A better approach is to make direct contact with those who hire or supervise people with your skills and ask them for an interview, even if no openings exist now. Then send a resume.

For an Electronic Resume, a Simple Design Is Best

The databases that your resume goes into want only text, not design. Scanners introduce fewer errors when the text is simple. What this means is that your resume's carefully done format and design elements need to be taken out, and your resume reduced to the simplest text format. Follow these guidelines:

- No graphics
- No lines
- No bold, italic, or other text variations

Electronic Resume

The sample resume has been rewritten from a traditional "on-paper" format to one for scanning or e-mail submission. It has a plain look that is easily read by scanners and key words that increase its chances of being selected in a search. This resume is based on one from Cyberspace Resume Kit *by Mary Nemnich and Fred Jandt (JIST Works).*

RICHARD JONES

3456 Generic Street

Potomac MD 11721

Phone messages: (301) 927-1189

E-mail: richj@riverview.com

[handwritten: Format to be scanned or e-mailed. No bold, bullets, or italics.]

[handwritten: Lots of key words to help get selected by computer searches by employers.]

SUMMARY OF SKILLS

Rigger, maintenance mechanic (carpentry, electrical, plumbing, painting), work leader. Read schematic diagrams. Flooring (wood, linoleum, carpet, ceramic and vinyl tile). Plumbing (pipes, fixtures, fire systems). Certified crane and forklift operator, work planner, inspector.

+++

EXPERIENCE *[handwritten: Includes results statements and numbers below.]*

Total of nine years in the trades—apprentice to work leader.

* MAINTENANCE MECHANIC LEADER, Smithsonian Institution, Washington, DC, April 2001 to present: Promoted to supervise nine staff in all trades, including plumbing, painting, electrical, carpentry, drywall, flooring. Prioritize and schedule work. Inspect and approve completed jobs. Responsible for annual budget of $750,000 and assuring that all work done to museum standards and building codes.

* RIGGER / MAINTENANCE MECHANIC, Smithsonian Institution, February 1998 to April 2001: Built and set up exhibits. Operated cranes, rollers, forklifts, and rigged mechanical and hydraulic systems to safely move huge, priceless museum exhibits. Worked with other trades in carpentry, plumbing, painting, electrical and flooring to construct exhibits.

* RIGGER APPRENTICE, Portsmouth Naval Shipyard, Portsmouth, NH, August 1996 to January 1998: Qualified signalman for cranes. Moved and positioned heavy machines and structural parts for shipbuilding. Responsible for safe operation of over $2,000,000 of equipment on a daily basis, with no injury or accidents. Used cranes, skids, rollers, jacks, forklifts and other equipment.

+++

TRAINING AND EDUCATION

HS graduate, top 50% of class.

Additional training in residential electricity, drywall, HV/AC, and refrigeration systems. Certified in heavy crane operation, forklift, regulated waste disposal, industrial blueprints.

- Only one easy-to-scan font

- No tab indentations

- No line or paragraph indents

- No centering; align text to the left

This may be discouraging, but it's the way it is.

The Requirements of One Large Employer Are Typical

Employers want resumes in electronic or scannable form to save time. It's not practical to look through hundreds or thousands of paper resumes. For this reason, Internet resume sites and many employers require you to submit your resume in a way that can be easily put into their databases. To show you how this works, I have included the following instructions from one large employer's Web site on how to submit a resume (see page 83). I've deleted references to the specific employer.

While these instructions aren't friendly, the reason for submitting a resume this way is pretty clear: No matter how you send your resume to the company, the company will convert the resume into a simple text file, and a machine will probably read it before a human being does.

Quick Tips to Reformat Your Paper Resume

Fortunately, you can easily take your existing resume and reformat it for electronic submission. Here are some quick tips for doing so:

1. Cut and paste your resume text into a new file in your word processor.

2. Eliminate any graphic elements, such as lines or images.

3. Set your margins so that text is no more than 65 characters wide.

4. Use one easy-to-scan font, such as Courier, Arial, Helvetica, or Times Roman. Eliminate bold, italic, and other font styles.

5. Introduce major sections with words in all uppercase letters, rather than in bold or a different font.

Instructions from a Large Employer
on How to Submit Your Resume

We are employing a new electronic applicant tracking system that uses the latest in document-imaging/scanning technology. The system allows us to receive your resume by e-mail, direct line fax, or hard copy. This system will enhance your exposure to a wider variety of employment opportunities at all sites within our company. The one-time submission of your resume makes you eligible for consideration of any openings for which you meet the minimum qualifications.

As your resume is input into our system, you receive an acknowledgment and your resume is kept active in our database for one year. As openings occur, our recruiters search the database for individuals whose qualifications and skills match the criteria needed for the open positions. If a match occurs, you receive further notification regarding the specific opening.

To increase the effectiveness of your resume, be sure to clearly state your skills and experiences, educational background, work history, and specific salary information. In addition, please follow these directions when preparing your resume:

◆ Prepare your resume on white or light-colored 8½-by-11 paper (hard copy or faxing).

◆ Please use a standard paper weight so that the system will produce a quality image (if hard copy or faxing).

◆ Avoid fancy treatments such as italics, underlining, and shadowing. Bold-faced type and capital letters are acceptable.

◆ Place your name at the top of the page on its own line, use a standard address format below your name, and list each phone number on a separate line.

You may submit your resume by one of the following methods:

◆ **Electronic mail.** The e-mail address is resume@bigcompany.com. You must put the word resume in the subject or reference line when e-mailing and submit it in ASCII text format. All information must be contained in the body of the message. We cannot accept attachments into this system.

◆ **Fax.** You may fax your information to 866-244-3325 (TOO-BIG-DEAL). Please fax in fine mode.

◆ **Postal mail.** You may mail a hard copy of your resume to Corporate Recruit-ment, Big Company, Corporate Center, Big City, TX 90214.

6. Keep all text aligned to the left and eliminate centering, unless you use the space key to do so.

7. Use a standard keyboard character, such as the asterisk, instead of using special symbols as bullets.

8. Use the space key to indent, instead of using the tab key or paragraph indents.

9. When done, click the File menu, choose the Save As command, and select the Plain Text, ASCII (American Standard Code for Information Interchange), or Text Only option.

10. Name the file and click Save or OK.

11. Reopen the file to see how it looks. Make additional format changes as needed.

While this reformatting may undermine your creative side, think of it as mashed potatoes: It can be very good if you do it right.

◆

A Few Final Words on Resumes

Before you write and use your resume, here is some advice that applies to both paper and electronic resumes:

◆ **Even the best of resumes will not get you a job.**

You have to do that yourself. To do so, you have to get interviews and do well in them. Interviews are where the job search action is, not resumes.

◆ **Don't listen to resume experts.**

If you ask 10 people for advice on your resume, they will all be willing to give it—yet no 2 will agree. You have to make up your own mind about your resume. Feel free to break any "rules," if you have a good reason.

◆ **Don't avoid the job search by worrying about your resume.**

Write a simple and error-free resume, and then go out and get lots of interviews. Later, you can write a better resume—if you want or need to.

◆ **Look over the sample resumes.**

I include several sample resumes at the end of this chapter. Some break "rules," and none are perfect. However, all are based on real resumes written by real people, although the names and other details have been changed. So look them over, learn from them, and then write your own.

◆

How to Write Effective Cover Letters

A cover letter is sent with and "covers" a resume. Different situations need different types of letters. As always, make certain that your correspondence makes a good impression.

You may find that you don't need to send many formal cover letters. Job seekers using the approaches I recommend get by with informal thank-you notes sent with resumes and JIST Cards. But certain types of jobs and some organizations require a more formal approach. Use your judgment.

The sample cover letters that follow deal with a variety of typical situations. Look them over for ideas to use when writing your own letters.

Some Tips for Writing and Using Superior Cover Letters

Here are some suggestions to help you create and use superior cover letters.

Target Your Letter

Typical reasons for sending a cover letter include responding to an ad, preparing an employer for an interview (the best reason!), and following up after a phone call or interview. Each of these letters is different.

Samples for each situation are included with the sample letters.

Send It to Someone by Name

Get the name of the person who is most likely to supervise you. Call first to get an interview. Then send your letter and resume.

Get It Right

Make sure you get the person's name, organization name, and address right. Include the person's correct job title. Make sure that your letter does not contain grammar and other errors; this creates a poor impression.

Be Clear About What You Want

If you want an interview, ask for it. If you are interested in the organization, say so. Give clear reasons why the company should consider you.

Be Friendly and Professional

A professional, informal style is usually best. Avoid a hard-sell "Hire-me-now!" approach. No one likes to be pushed.

Make It Look Good

Just like a resume, correspondence to an employer must look good. Use good-quality paper and matching envelopes. A standard business format is good for most letters.

Follow Up

Remember that contacting an employer directly is much more effective than sending a letter. Don't expect letters to get you many interviews. They are best used to follow up after you have contacted the employer.

Cover Letter for a Specific Opening

This new graduate called first and arranged an interview—the best approach of all. She mentions specifically how she changed procedures for a business and saved money. Note how she includes skills such as working hard and dealing with deadline pressure.

113 S. Meridian Street
Greenwich, Connecticut 11721

March 10, 20XX

Ms. Willa Hines
New England Power and Light Company
604 Waterway Boulevard
Parien, Connecticut 11716

Dear Ms. Hines:

I am following up on the brief chat we had today by phone. After getting the details on the position you have open, I am certain that it is the kind of job I have been looking for. A copy of my resume is enclosed providing more details of my background. I hope you have a chance to review it before we meet next week.

My special interest has long been in the large-volume order processing systems that your organization has developed so well. While in school I researched the flow of order processing work for a large corporation as part of a class assignment. With some simple and inexpensive procedural changes I recommended, check-processing time was reduced by an average of three days. For the number of checks and dollars involved, this one change resulted in an estimated increase in interest revenues of over $135,000 per year.

While I have recently graduated from business school, I have considerable experience for a person of my age. I have worked in a variety of jobs dealing with large numbers of people and deadline pressure. My studies have also been far more hands-on and practical than those of most schools, so I have a good working knowledge of current business systems and procedures. This includes a good understanding of various computer spreadsheet and application programs, the use of automation, and experience with cutting costs and increasing profits. I am also a hard worker and realize I will need to apply myself to get established in my career.

I am most interested in the position you have available and am excited about the potential it offers. I look forward to seeing you next week.

Sincerely,

Wendy Presson

Cover Letter After an Interview

The writer uncovered a problem during an interview and afterward offers to solve the problem when no job exists. Many job seekers never think of scheduling an interview when there is no job opening, but many jobs are created this way to accommodate a good person.

Sandra A. Zaremba

115 South Hawthorn Drive
Dunwoody, Georgia 21599

April 10, XXXX

Ms. Christine Massey
Import Distributors, Inc.
417 East Main Street
Atlanta, Georgia 21649

Dear Ms. Massey:

I know you have a busy schedule so I was pleasantly surprised when you arranged a time for me to see you. While you don't have a position open now, your organization is just the sort of place I would like to work. As we discussed, I like to be busy with a variety of duties and the active pace I saw at your company is what I seek.

Your ideas on increasing business sound creative. I've thought about the customer service problem and would like to discuss a possible solution. It would involve the use of a simple system of color-coded files that would prioritize correspondence to give older requests priority status. The handling of complaints could also be speeded up through the use of simple form letters similar to those you mentioned. I have some thoughts on how this might be done too, and I will work out a draft of procedures and sample letters if you are interested. It can be done on the computers your staff already uses and would not require any additional cost to implement.

Whether or not you have a position for me in the future, I appreciate the time you have given me. An extra copy of my resume is enclosed for your files—or to pass on to someone else.

Let me know if you want to discuss the ideas I presented earlier in this letter. I can be reached at any time on my cell phone at (942) 267-1103. I will call you next week, as you suggested, to keep you informed of my progress.

Sincerely,

Sandra A. Zaremba

Cover Letter from a Network Contact

The person uses names from a professional association to conduct a long-distance job search. He explains the end of his old job, indicates certain skills, and mentions the availability of positive references. He also requests an interview even though no job may be open.

July 10, XXXX

Mr. Paul Resley
Operations Manager
Rollem Trucking Co.
I-70 Freeway Drive
Kansas City, Missouri 78401

Mr. Resley:

I obtained your name from the membership directory of the Affiliated Trucking Association. I have been a member for over 10 years, and I am very active in the Southeast Region. The reason I am writing is to ask for your help. The firm I had been employed with has been bought by a larger corporation. The operations here have been disbanded, leaving me unemployed.

While I like where I live, I know that finding a position at the level of responsibility I seek may require a move. As a center of the transportation business, your city is one I have targeted for special attention. A copy of my resume is enclosed for your use. I'd like you to review it and consider where a person with my background would get a good reception in Kansas City. Perhaps you could think of a specific person for me to contact?

I have specialized in fast-growing organizations or ones that have experienced rapid change. My particular strength is in bringing things under control, then increasing profits. While my resume does not state this, I have excellent references from my former employer and would have stayed if a similar position existed at its new location.

As a member of the association, I hoped that you would provide some special attention to my request for assistance. I plan on coming to Kansas City on a job-hunting trip within the next six weeks. Prior to my trip I will call you for advice on who I might contact for interviews. Even if they have no jobs open for me now, perhaps they will know of someone else who does.

My enclosed resume lists my phone number and other contact information should you want to reach me before I call you. Thanks in advance for your help on this.

Sincerely,

John B. Goode
Treasurer, Southeast Region
Affiliated Trucking Association

John B. Goode

312 Smokie Way   Nashville, Tennessee 31201

Cover Letter Following Up on a Cold Call

This person made contact with the office manager by phone and set up an interview for his upcoming visit to the area.

1768 South Carrollton Street
Nashville, Tennessee 96050
May 26, XXXX

Ms. Karen Miller
Office Manager
Lendon, Lendon, and Sears
Suite 101, Landmark Building
Summit, New Jersey 11736

Dear Ms. Miller:

Enclosed is a copy of my resume that describes my work experience as a legal assistant. I hope this information will be helpful as background for our interview next Monday at 4 p.m.

I appreciate your taking time to describe your requirements so fully. This sounds like a position that could develop into a satisfying career. And my training in accounting—along with experience using a variety of computer programs—seems to match your needs.

Lendon, Lendon, and Sears is a highly respected name in New Jersey. I am excited about this opportunity and I look forward to meeting with you.

Sincerely,

Richard Wittenberg

More Sample Resumes

The sample resumes that follow give you content, style, and format ideas. Space limited the number of samples I could include. The ones I do include use pretty simple formats. Professional resume writers created some of these resumes, and their names are noted at the bottoms of those examples. You can find professional resume writers in your area through the Professional Association of Résumé Writers and Career Coaches at www.parw.com and the National Résumé Writers' Association at www.nrwa.com.

If you want to see more resumes, many good books and Web sites provide samples. JIST publishes excellent resume collections written by professional resume writers. And I've written several resume books that provide lots of examples.

Quip

Keep competitive with two resumes.

As use of electronic resumes and scanning increases, it makes sense to have two resumes: one on paper that looks good to humans and another that scans and e-mails well. Having both, for use in different situations, gives you a competitive edge.

Chronological Resume Stresses Technical Credentials

This resume emphasizes Jack's technical qualifications. The Additional Qualifications section highlights statements that do not fit into a traditional chronological form.

Chronological resume with some nice features that make it very effective.

Simple but attractive use of bold, centering, and lines.

Jack B. Harris

12 Browertown Road   Little Falls, NJ 07424   Messages: (201) 785-3011
                          e-mail: Jbquick@autonet.com

Class A Automotive Mechanic
Specializing in complete engine overhaul and front end repair work

Education & Training

Graduate of Rockford Community College, 1998
Basic and Advanced Automotive Technology courses. Top 20% of class.
ASE Certified in repair of:

- Engines
- Suspensions
- Steering
- Cooling systems
- Brakes
- Electrical systems

GM training on the job:
- Use of computerized engine analyzers and other electronic test devices.
- Diagnostics and service to electronic fuel injection, ignition, and emission control components.

Additional Qualifications

This section includes details that would not be easy to list in a typical chronological format.

- Experience with foreign and domestic late model cars, vans and light trucks.
- Stay current on new technology; understand and act on instructions from repair manuals and manufacturers' bulletins.
- Very service oriented, hard working and cooperative.
- Own power and hand tools for most applications; able to do heavy lifting.

Strong, direct words emphasize effectiveness and results.

Work Experience

2000–Present   **Master Automotive Technician**
                      DRISCOLL CHEVROLET, South Caldwell, NJ

- Attained highest status at dealership employing 12 technicians because of ability to quickly diagnose troubles and make accurate repairs.
- Kept track of recurring problems in certain models for manufacturer notification. Shared information with other mechanics.
- Increased department profitability by consistently performing most services in 10-20% less time than allowed by industry standards.
- Contributed to 29% increase in customer satisfaction levels over the last year.

Numbers support his results and skills.

1997-2000   **Automotive Mechanic**
                   SEARS AUTO CENTER, Clairmont, NJ

- Started with basic tune-ups and tire service, advancing after 2 months to brake, general repair, radiator and air conditioning repairs.
- Was often assigned to customers with complaints of unsatisfactory original service. Corrected problems and maintained good relationships.
- Trained 6 newly hired mechanics in shop procedures.

Chronological section - notice the use of check marks. Much better than a paragraph of text!

Submitted by Melanie A. Noonan

Chronological Resume Emphasizes Results

A simple format emphasizes Maria's accomplishments through the use of numbers. While her resume does not say so, it is obvious that she works hard and that she gets results.

A simple chronological format with few but carefully chosen words. It has an effective Summary at the beginning, and every word supports her job objective.

She emphasizes results!

Maria Marquez

4141 Beachway Road
Redondo Beach, California 90277

Messages: (213) 432-2279
E-mail: mmarq@msn.net

Objective: Management Position in a Major Hotel

Summary of Experience: Four years' experience in sales, catering, banquet services, and guest relations in 300-room hotel. Doubled sales revenues from conferences and meetings. Increased dining room and bar revenues by 44%. Won prestigious national and local awards for increased productivity and services.

Experience: Park Regency Hotel, Los Angeles, California
Assistant Manager
1999 to Present

- Oversee a staff of 36 including dining room and bar, housekeeping, and public relations operations.
- Introduced new menus and increased dining room revenues by 44%. Gourmet America awarded us their first place Hotel Haute Cuisine award as a result of my efforts.
- Attracted 28% more diners with the first revival of Big Band Cocktail Dances in the Los Angeles area.

Kingsmont Hotel, Redondo Beach, California
Sales and Public Relations
1997 to 1999

- Doubled revenues per month from conferences and meetings.
- Redecorated meeting rooms and updated sound and visual media equipment. Careful scheduling resulted in no lost revenue during this time.
- Instituted staff reward program, which resulted in an upgrade from B- to AAA+ in the *Car and Travel Handbook*.

Education: Associate Degree in Hotel Management from Henfield College of San Francisco. One-year certification program with the Boileau Culinary Institute, where I won the Grand Prize Scholarship.

Notice her use of numbers to increase impact of statements

Bullets here and above increase readability and emphasis.

While Maria had only a few years of related work experience, she used this resume to help her land a very responsible job in a large resort hotel.

Skills Resume for Someone with Limited Work Experience

This resume is for a recent high school graduate whose only paid work experience was at a fast-food restaurant.

A skills resume where each skill directly supports the job objective of this recent high school graduate with very limited work experience.

Lisa M. Rhodes
813 Lava Court • Denver, Colorado 81613
Home: (413) 643-2173 (leave message)
Cell phone: (413) 442-1659
Email: lrhodes@netcom.net

Position Desired

Sales-oriented position in a retail sales or distribution business.

Support for the skills comes from all life activities: school, clubs, part-time jobs.

Skills and Abilities

Key skills

Communications
Good written and verbal presentation skills. Use proper grammar and have a good speaking voice.

Interpersonal
Able to get along well with coworkers and accept supervision. Received positive evaluations from previous supervisors.

← Good emphasis on adaptive skills.

Flexible
Willing to try new things and am interested in improving efficiency on assigned tasks.

Attention to Detail
Concerned with quality. My work is typically orderly and attractive. Like to see things completed correctly and on time.

Hard Working
Throughout high school, worked long hours in strenuous activities while attending school full-time. Often handled as many as 65 hours a week in school and other structured activities, while maintaining above-average grades.

Very strong statement.

Customer Contacts
Routinely handled as many as 500 customer contacts a day (10,000 per month) in a busy retail outlet. Averaged less than a .001% complaint rate and was given the "Employee of the Month" award in my second month of employment. Received two merit increases. Never absent or late.

Good use of numbers

Cash Sales
Handled over $2,000 a day ($40,000 a month) in cash sales. Balanced register and prepared daily sales summary and deposits.

Reliable
Excellent attendance record, trusted to deliver daily cash deposits totaling over $40,000 a month.

Education

Franklin High School. Took advanced English and other classes. Member of award-winning band. Excellent attendance record. Superior communication skills. Graduated in top 30% of class.

Other

Active gymnastics competitor for four years. This taught me discipline, teamwork, how to follow instructions, and hard work. I am ambitious, outgoing, reliable, and willing to work.

Lisa's resume makes it clear that she is talented and hard working.

Combination Resume for a Career Changer

Because this job seeker has no work experience in the computer programming field, this resumes focuses on her relevant education and transferable skills.

Writer's comments: This client was finishing computer programming school and had no work experience in the field. After listing the topics covered in the course, I summarized her employment experience, specifying that she earned promotions quickly. This **Mary Beth Kurzak** *would be attractive to any employer.*

2188 Huron River Drive • Ann Arbor, MI 48104 • 734-555-4912

Profile
➤ Strong educational preparation with practical applications in computer/internet programming.
➤ Highly motivated to excel in new career.
➤ A fast learner, as evidenced by success in accelerated training program.
➤ Self-directed, independent worker with proven ability to meet deadlines and work under pressure.
➤ Maintain team perspective with ability to build positive working relationships and foster open communication.

Education/Training
ADVANCED TECHNOLOGY CENTER • Dearborn, MI   xxxx-Present
Pursuing Certification in **Internet/Information Technology**   *Anticipated completion: Aug. xxxx*
An accelerated program focusing on computer and internet programming.
Highlights of Training:

Important to include specific things learned →

- Networking Concepts	- Client Server	- UNIX
- Programming Concepts	- Visual Basic	- IIS
- Programming in Java/Java Script	- C/C++	- VB/ASP
- Web Authoring Using HTML	- Oracle	- CGI
- Photoshop	- DHTML, XML	- Perl

Highlights of Experience and Abilities

Experiences selected to support job objective

Customer Service
➤ Determined member eligibility and verified policy benefits.
➤ Responded to customer questions; interpreted and explained complex insurance concepts.
➤ Collaborated with health care providers regarding billing and claim procedures.

Leadership
➤ Creatively supervised 30 employees, many of whom were significantly older.
➤ Motivated employees and improved working conditions, resulting in greater camaraderie.
➤ Trained coworkers in various technical and nontechnical processes.

Analytical/Troubleshooting
➤ Investigated and resolved computer system errors.
➤ Researched discrepancies in claims and identified appropriate actions.
➤ Compiled and analyzed claims statistics.

Administrative Support and Accounting
➤ Managed and processed medical, mental health and substance abuse claims.
➤ Oversaw accounts receivable; reconciled receipts and prepared bank deposits.
➤ Coordinated 50+ line switchboard; routed calls as appropriate.

Employment History
MEDICAL SERVICES PLUS [Contracted by Health Solutions - Southfield, MI]   xxxx-xxxx
Promoted within eight months of hire.
Claims Supervisor / Claims Adjudicator

HANSEN AGENCY OF MICHIGAN • Ann Arbor, MI   xxxx-xxxx
Earned two promotions in one year.
Claims Adjudicator / Accounting Clerk / Receptionist

FORD WILLOW RUN TRANSMISSION PLANT • Ypsilanti, MI   Summer xxxx
Temporary Production Worker

PEARL HARBOR MEMORIAL MUSEUM • Pearl Harbor, HI   xxxx-xxxx
Assistant Crew Manager

References available on request

Submitted by Janet L. Beckstrom

Combination Resume with Matching JIST Card

This resume showcases the job seeker's substantial work experience. He emphasizes skills related to his job objective in the first section and then includes his work history in chronological form later. Peter's JIST Card shows how these two job search tools can relate to each other effectively.

Carefully written combination resume includes both skills and chronological sections.

Peter Neely

203 Evergreen Road
Houston, Texas 39127
Messages: (237) 649-1234   Pager: (237) 765-9876

POSITION DESIRED: Short- or Long-Distance Truck Driver

Summary of Work Experience:	Over fifteen years of stable work history, including substantial experience with diesel engines, electrical systems, and driving all sorts of trucks and heavy equipment.

SKILLS ← *Skills format allows him to stress experiences that are important for the job*

Driving Record/ Licenses:	Have current Commercial Driving License and Chauffeur's License and am qualified and able to drive anything that rolls. <u>No traffic citations</u> or accidents for over 20 years.
Vehicle Maintenance:	I maintain correct maintenance schedules and <u>avoid most breakdowns</u> as a result. <u>Substantial mechanical and electrical systems training</u> and experience permit many breakdowns to be repaired immediately and <u>avoid towing.</u>
Record Keeping:	Excellent <u>attention to detail.</u> Familiar with recording procedures and submit required records on a <u>timely basis.</u>
Routing:	Thorough knowledge of most major interstate routes, with <u>good map reading and route planning skills.</u> I tend to get <u>there on time and without incident.</u>
Other:	Not afraid of hard work, <u>flexible, get along well with others, meet deadlines, excellent attendance, responsible.</u>

Lots of emphasis on reliability and results.

Key adaptive skills

WORK EXPERIENCE

Short chronological listings reinforce his good work history

1999—Present	CAPITAL TRUCK CENTER, Houston, Texas Pick up and deliver all types of commercial vehicles from across the United States. Am <u>trusted with handling large sums of money</u> and handling complex truck purchasing transactions.
1995—1999	QUALITY PLATING CO., Houston, Texas Promoted from production to Quality Control. Developed numerous <u>production improvements</u> resulting in <u>substantial cost savings.</u>
1992—1995	BLUE CROSS MANUFACTURING, Houston, Texas Received several <u>increases in salary and responsibility</u> before leaving for a more challenging position.
Prior to 1992	Truck delivery of food products to destinations throughout the South. Also responsible for up to 12 drivers and equipment maintenance personnel.

Summarizes "old" experience

OTHER

No dates on older military experience, but emphasizes related skills.

Four years' experience in the U.S. Air Force, driving and operating truck-mounted diesel power plants. Responsible for monitoring and maintenance on a rigid 24-hour schedule. Stationed in Alaska, California, Wyoming, and other states. Honorable discharge.

High school graduate plus training in diesel engines and electrical systems. Excellent health, love the outdoors, stable family life, nonsmoker and nondrinker.

Peter Neely

Messages: (237) 649-1234
Pager: (237) 765-9876

Position: Short- or Long-Distance Truck Driver

Background and Skills: Over fifteen years of stable work history including no traffic citations or accidents. Formal training in diesel mechanics and electrical systems. Familiar with most major destinations and have excellent map-reading and problem-solving abilities. I can handle responsibility and have a track record of getting things done.

Excellent health, good work history, dependable

Chronological Resumes with Unique Graphic Touches

These two resumes show how simple graphic images can convey a job objective and make a resume stand out in a crowd. Both also feature lots of white space for easy reading.

Writer's comments: Skip has limited broadcasting experience, so the challenge was to demonstrate his potential for success. The resume emphasizes Skip's production and on-air experience, stressing high-quality production, audience appeal and broad knowledge of many kinds of music. The graphic and fonts gave the resume the desired funky look.

Daniel "Skip" Norton
44 Buckingham Road • Allston, MA 02132 • (617) 555–5555

Summary

Over 5 years in broadcasting, including production, engineering, and on-air experience. Knowledge of extensive variety of music with appeal to broad range of listeners. Expertise in state-of-the art technology, including 24-track recording and digital editing. Ability to work well under pressure. Commitment to high standards of quality.

Related Experience

WZZX 92.9 FM Boston, MA   xxxx–present
Host, Producer, Engineer of six-hour weekly show called Daydream. Freeform format consisting of music from station's playlist and from extensive personal library and combining alternative and popular material.

- Expanded audience size by encouraging and increasing listener feedback.
- Successfully modified format to appeal to broader audience.
- Serve as substitute host for other shows, as needed.
- Maintain consistent, high standards of production by reviewing program tapes and responding to listener feedback.
- Introduce and feature new local artists.
- Produce promotional spots.

A very clean format with good use of white space

Boston Audio, Allston, MA   xxxx–present
Producer, Manager of my own project studio.

- Archive rare and odd records.
- Record material for promotions, including sound effects and music.
- Produce and record local artists for demos and release material.

Other Experience

Head Barista, Coffee Brewers, Newton, MA   xxxx–present
Assistant Manager, Coffee Specialties, Needham, MA   xxxx–xxxx

Education

Full Sail Center for the Recording Arts, Winter Park, FL   xxxx
Associate's Degree in Audio Engineering

Submitted by Wendy Gelberg

François J. Boudreau

88 Harbor Place
Rock Cove, ME 00000

(207) 555-5555

Objective:

Assistant or Sous Chef

Summary of Qualifications:

+ Associate's Degree in Culinary Arts with training in American and International Cuisines
+ Restaurant experience has included broiler, grill, sauté, fryer, expo, breakfast and salads
+ Able to handle a multitude of tasks at once, meeting deadlines under pressure
+ Demonstrates ability to respond with speed and accuracy in a highly productive setting
+ Works cooperatively and harmoniously with coworkers and supervisors
+ Dedicated to quality in service and product

Experience:

Broiler/Prep Cook   Jacques Restaurant, West Cove, Maine (9/94 to Present)
200-seat Four Diamond restaurant featuring an extensive menu of French and American cuisine

Fry Cook   The Lobster Net, Port Hancock, Maine (1992-94)
Indoor and outdoor dining, specializing in fresh lobsters and seafood; take-out and banquet service

Fry/Prep Cook   The Weathervane, Rocky Coast, Maine (1991)
Traditional New England seafood served in a casual setting

Education:

Associate's Degree in Culinary Arts – Newbury College, Brookline, Massachusetts (1992)
Curriculum and Training included:

◇ Soup, Stock and Sauces   ◇ American Cuisine
◇ Breads and Rolls   ◇ International Cuisine
◇ Desserts   ◇ Yarde Manger
◇ Classical Bakeshop   ◇ Sanitation and Dining Room

Submitted by Becky J. Davis

Redefine What Counts as an Interview, Then Organize Your Time to Get 2 a Day

The average job seeker gets about 5 interviews a month—fewer than 2 a week. Yet many job seekers use the methods in this book to get 2 interviews a day. Getting 2 interviews a day equals 10 a week and 40 a month. That's 800 percent more interviews than the average job seeker gets.

Who do you think will get a job offer quicker?

However, getting 2 interviews a day is nearly impossible unless you redefine what counts as an interview. If you consider an interview in a different way, getting 2 a day is quite possible.

THE NEW DEFINITION OF AN INTERVIEW

AN INTERVIEW IS ANY FACE-TO-FACE CONTACT WITH SOMEONE WHO HAS THE AUTHORITY TO HIRE OR SUPERVISE A PERSON WITH YOUR SKILLS— EVEN IF NO OPENING EXISTS AT THE TIME WHEN YOU INTERVIEW.

If you use this new definition, it becomes *much* easier to get interviews. You can now interview with all sorts of potential employers, not just those who have job openings now. While most other job seekers look for advertised or actual openings, you can get interviews before a job opens up or before it is advertised and widely known. You will be considered for jobs that may soon be created but that others will not know about. And, of course, you can also interview for existing openings as everyone else does.

Spending as much time as possible on your job search and setting a job search schedule are important parts of Step 5.

Make Your Search a Full-Time Job

Job seekers average fewer than 15 hours a week looking for work. On average, unemployment lasts three or more months, with some people out of work far longer (for example, older workers and higher earners).

My many years of experience researching job seekers indicates that, the more time you spend on your job search each week, the less time you will likely remain unemployed.

Of course, using the more effective job search methods presented in *Seven Steps to Getting a Job Fast* also helps. Many job search programs that teach job seekers my basic approach of using more effective methods and spending more time looking have proven that these seekers often find a job in half the average time. More importantly, many job seekers also find better jobs using these methods.

So, if you are unemployed and looking for a full-time job, you should plan to look on a full-time basis. It just makes sense to do so, although many do not, or they start out well but quickly get discouraged. Most job seekers simply don't have a structured plan—they have no idea what they are going to do next Thursday. The plan that follows will show you how to structure your job search like a job.

Decide How Much Time You Will Spend Looking for Work Each Week and Day

First and most importantly, decide how many hours you are willing to spend each week on your job search. You should spend a minimum of 25 hours a week on hard-core job search activities with no goofing around. Let me walk you through a simple but effective process to set a week's job search schedule.

PLAN YOUR JOB SEARCH WEEK

1. How many hours are you willing to spend each week looking for a job? _____

_____

---

2. Which days of the week will you spend looking for a job?

_____

_____

_____

3. How many hours will you look each day? _____

_____

_____

4. At what times will you begin and end your job search on each of these days? _____

_____

_____

_____

Create a Specific Daily Job Search Schedule

Having a specific daily schedule is essential because most job seekers find it hard to stay productive each day. The sample daily schedule that follows is the result of years of research into what schedule gets the best results. I tested many schedules in job search programs I ran, and this particular schedule worked best.

You can review the sample daily schedule for ideas on creating your own, but I urge you to consider using one like this.

Quip

Time is money.

The daily schedule you see on this page is based on my years of managing results-oriented job search programs. As simple as it seems, keeping a schedule like this will cut your job search time. Many thousands have used it as a basis for their daily job search plan, and it does work.

A Sample Daily Schedule That Works

Time	Activity
7 a.m.	Get up, shower, dress, eat breakfast.
8–8:15 a.m.	Organize work space, review schedule for today's interviews and promised follow-ups, update schedule as needed.
8:15–9 a.m.	Review old leads for follow-up needed today; develop new leads from want ads, yellow pages, the Internet, warm contact lists, and other sources; complete daily contact list.
9–10 a.m.	Make phone calls and set up interviews.
10–10:15 a.m.	Take a break.
10:15–11 a.m.	Make more phone calls, set up more interviews.
11 a.m.–Noon	Send follow-up notes and do other "office" activities as needed.
Noon–1 p.m.	Lunch break, relax.
1–3 p.m.	Go on interviews, make cold contacts in the field.
Evening	Read job search books, make calls to warm contacts not reachable during the day, work on a "better" resume, spend time with friends and family, exercise, relax.

DO IT NOW: GET A DAILY PLANNER AND CREATE A SPECIFIC DAILY SCHEDULE

IF YOU ARE NOT ACCUSTOMED TO USING A DAILY SCHEDULE BOOK OR ELECTRONIC PLANNER, PROMISE YOURSELF TO GET A GOOD ONE TOMORROW.

Choose one that allows plenty of space for each day's plan on an hourly basis, plus room for daily to-do lists. Write in your daily schedule in advance, and then add interviews as they come. Get used to carrying it with you and use it!

There are a variety of computer programs that can be used to help organize your job search. And pocket-sized schedulers can be very helpful. If you have these resources, adapt the advice I have provided in this step to use these tools. If you don't use electronic tools, a simple schedule book and other paper systems will work just fine.

Dramatically Improve Your Interviewing Skills

Interviews are where the job search action is. You have to get them; then you have to do well in them. According to surveys of employers, most job seekers do not effectively present the skills they have to do the job. Even worse, most job seekers can't answer one or more problem questions. This lack of performance in interviews is one reason why employers will often hire a job seeker who does well in the interview instead of someone with better credentials.

The good news is that you can do simple things to dramatically improve your interviewing skills. This section will emphasize interviewing tips and techniques that make the most difference.

Your First Impression May Be the Only One You Make

Some research suggests that, if the interviewer forms a negative impression in the first five minutes of an interview, your chances of getting a job offer approach zero. I know from experience that many job seekers can create a lasting negative impression in seconds.

A positive first impression is so important—here are some suggestions to help you get off to a good start:

◆ **Dress and groom like the interviewer is likely to be dressed—but cleaner!**

Employer surveys find that almost half of all people's dress or grooming create an initial negative impression. So this is a *big* problem. If necessary, get advice on your interviewing outfits from someone who dresses well. Pay close attention to your grooming, too. Little things do count.

- ◆ **Be early.**

  Leave in plenty of time to be a few minutes early to an interview.

- ◆ **Be friendly and respectful with the receptionist.**

  Doing otherwise will often get back to the interviewer and result in a quick rejection.

- ◆ **Follow the interviewer's lead in the first few minutes.**

  It's often informal small talk but very important for that person to see how you interact. This is a good time to make a positive comment on the organization or even something you see in the office.

- ◆ **Do some homework on the organization before you go.**

  You can often get information on a business and on industry trends from the Internet or a library.

- ◆ **Make a good impression before you arrive.**

  Your resume, e-mails, applications, and other written correspondence create an impression before the interview, so make them professional and error free.

A Traditional Interview Is Not a Friendly Exchange

In a traditional interview situation, there is a job opening, and you will be one of several who've applied for it. In this setting, the employer's task is to eliminate all applicants but one. The interviewer's questions are designed to elicit information that can be used to screen you out. And your objective is to avoid getting screened out. It's hardly an open and honest interaction, is it?

This illustrates yet another advantage of setting up interviews before an opening exists. This eliminates the stress of a traditional interview. Employers are not trying to screen you out, and you are not trying to keep them from finding out stuff about you.

Having said that, knowing how to answer questions that might be asked in a traditional interview is good preparation for any interview you face.

How to Answer Tough Interview Questions

Your answers to a few key problem questions may determine if you get a job offer. There are simply too many possible interview questions to cover one by one. Instead, the 10 basic questions that follow cover variations of most other interview questions. So, if you can learn to answer these 10 questions well, you will know how to answer most others.

Top 10 Problem Interview Questions

1. Why should I hire you?

2. Why don't you tell me about yourself?

3. What are your major strengths?

4. What are your major weaknesses?

5. What sort of pay do you expect to receive?

6. How does your previous experience relate to the jobs we have here?

7. What are your plans for the future?

8. What will your former employer (or references) say about you?

9. Why are you looking for this type of position, and why here?

10. Why don't you tell me about your personal situation?

The Three-Step Process for Answering Interview Questions

I know this might seem too simple, but the three-step process is easy to remember and can help you create a good answer to most interview questions. The technique has worked for thousands of people, so consider trying it. The three steps are

1. Understand what is really being asked.

2. Answer the question briefly.

3. Answer the real concern.

Step 1. Understand what is really being asked.

Most questions are designed to find out about your self-management skills and personality, but interviewers are rarely this blunt. The employer's *real* question is often one or more of the following:

Can I depend on you?

Are you easy to get along with?

Are you a good worker?

Do you have the experience and training to do the job if we hire you?

Are you likely to stay on the job for a reasonable period of time and be productive?

Ultimately, if you don't convince the employer that you will stay and be a good worker, it won't matter if you have the best credentials—he or she won't hire you.

Step 2. Answer the question briefly.

Present the facts of your particular work experience, but...*present them as advantages, not disadvantages.*

Many interview questions encourage you to provide negative information. One classic question I included in my list of Top 10 Problem Interview Questions was "What are your major weaknesses?" This is obviously a trick question, and many people are just not prepared for it.

A good response is to mention something that is not very damaging, such as *"I have been told that I am a perfectionist, sometimes not delegating as effectively as I might."*

However, your answer is not complete until you continue with Step 3.

Step 3. Answer the real concern by presenting your related skills.

Base your answer on the key skills you have that support the job, and give examples to support these skills.

In the previous example (about failing to delegate as a weakness), a good skills statement that addresses the interviwer's real concern might be the following:

"I've been working on this problem and have learned to let my staff do more, making sure that they have good training and supervision. I've found that their performance improves, and it frees me up to do other things."

In another scenario, an employer might say to a recent graduate, *"We were looking for someone with more experience in this field. Why should we consider you?"* Here is one possible answer:

"I'm sure there are people who have more experience, but I do have more than six years of work experience including three years of advanced training and hands-on experience using the latest methods and techniques. Because my training is recent, I am open to new ideas and am used to working hard and learning quickly."

Whatever your situation, learn to answer questions that present you well. It's essential to communicate your skills during an interview, and the three-step process can help you answer problem questions and dramatically improve your responses. It works!

The Most Important Interview Question of All: "Why Should I Hire You?"

This is the most important question to answer well. Do you have a convincing argument why someone should hire you over someone else? If you don't, you probably won't get that job you really want. So think carefully about why someone *should* hire you and practice your response. Then, make sure you communicate this in the interview, even if the interviewer never asks the question in a clear way.

Tips on Negotiating Pay—How to Earn a Thousand Dollars a Minute

The following statements are NOT recommended ways to start negotiating for pay:

"I can't even discuss the job before I know if you'll meet my price range."

"I really don't care about money…"

"What do you think I'm worth?"

"My bottom line is $45,000, plus an expense account."

"Well, I'd LIKE $3 billion, but you probably can't afford me. Ha, ha…"

"I made $30,00 a year in my last job. Can you match that?"

"I'll work for any amount. I just need a job."

When it comes time to negotiate your pay, the above tactics won't work. Instead, remember these few essential ideas:

THE ONLY TIME TO NEGOTIATE IS AFTER YOU HAVE BEEN OFFERED THE JOB.

Employers want to know how much you want to be paid so that they can eliminate you from consideration. They figure, if you want too much, you won't be happy with their job and won't stay. And, if you will take too little, they may think you don't have enough experience. So *never* discuss your salary expectations until an employer offers you the job.

IF PRESSED, SPEAK IN TERMS OF WIDE PAY RANGES.

If you are pushed to reveal your pay expectations early in an interview, ask the interviewer what the normal pay range is for this job. Interviewers will often tell you, and you can say that you would consider offers in this range.

If you are forced to be more specific, speak in terms of a wide pay range. For example, if you figure that the company will likely pay from $20,000 to $25,000 a year, say that you would consider "any fair offer in the low to mid-twenties." This statement covers the employer's range *and goes a bit higher*. If all else fails, tell the interviewer that you would consider any reasonable offer.

For this to work, you must know in advance what the job is likely to pay. You can get this information by asking people who do similar work, or from a variety of books and Internet sources of career information.

Close the Interview Effectively

Most interviews simply end with a fizzle, but there are some things you can do while an interview is ending that can make a difference. Even if you are not certain you want this job, it is wise to go after a job offer—you can always turn it down later. And, it is quite possible that there are other jobs with the same employer, if the interviewer likes you.

♦ **Emphasize your key skills.**

Tell the interviewer why they should hire you over someone else by reviewing the skills you have to do this job.

♦ **Ask for the job.**

If you do want the job, say so. Employers want to hire people who are enthusiastic about doing the sort of work they need done.

♦ **Arrange to call back.**

Ask for a specific time and date to call the employer back and ask questions or learn of your status.

Don't Say "No" Too Quickly

Never, ever turn down a job offer during an interview! Instead, thank the interviewer for the offer and ask to consider the offer overnight. You can turn it down tomorrow, saying how much you appreciate the offer and asking to be considered for other jobs that pay better or whatever.

But, this is no time to be playing games. If you want the job, you should say so. And it is okay to ask for additional pay or other concessions. But if you simply can't accept the offer, say why and ask the interviewer to keep you in mind for future opportunities. You just never know.

Follow Up on All Job Leads

It's a fact: People who follow up with potential employers and with others in their network get jobs faster than those who do not. Here are a few rules to guide you in your job search.

Four Rules for Effective Follow-Up

1. Send a thank-you note or e-mail to every person who helps you in your job search.

2. Send the note within 24 hours after speaking with the person.

3. Enclose JIST Cards with thank-you notes and all other correspondence.

4. Develop a system to keep following up with good contacts.

Thank-You Notes Make a Difference

While thank-you notes can be e-mailed, most people appreciate and are more impressed by a mailed note. Here are some tips about mailed thank-you notes that you can easily adapt to e-mail use.

Thank-you notes can be handwritten or typed on quality paper and matching envelopes. Keep them simple, neat, and error free. And make sure to include a few copies of your JIST Cards. An example of a simple thank-you note follows.

Sample Thank-You Note

2244 Riverwood Avenue
Philadelphia, PA 17963
April 16, XXXX

Ms. Helen A. Colcord
Henderson & Associates, Inc.
1801 Washington Blvd., Suite 1201
Philadelphia, PA 17993

Dear Ms. Colcord:

Thank you for sharing your time with me so generously today. I really appreciated seeing your state-of-the-art computer equipment.

Your advice has already proved helpful. I have an appointment to meet with Mr. Robert Hopper on Friday. As you anticipated, he does intend to add more computer operators in the next few months.

In case you think of someone else who might need a person like me, I'm enclosing another JIST Card. I will let you know how the interview with Mr. Hopper goes.

Sincerely,

William Henderson

William Henderson

Develop an Organized System for Following Up

If you use contact management software, use it to schedule follow-up activities. Pocket schedulers and organizers can also be very helpful to remind you of interviews and things to do. A simple paper system can work very well also or can be adapted for setting up your contact management software.

Following are a few ideas to help you follow up more effectively.

Use Job Lead Cards

By using the job search methods you have learned in this book, you can develop hundreds of contacts. Keeping track of them is more than any person's memory can handle.

Look at the following sample job lead card. It shows the kind of information you can keep about each person who helps you in your job search. (If desired, you can list the same kind of information in a computer database.)

To start such a system, buy a few hundred 3-by-5-inch cards. Create one job lead card for every person who gives you a referral or who is a possible employer. Keep brief notes each time you talk with that person, to help you remember important details for your next contact. Notice that the notes on the sample card are short, but they contain enough data to help the job seeker remember what happened and when to follow up.

Organization: **Mutual Health Insurance**

Contact person: **Anna Tomey**

Phone number: **(555) 555-2211**

Source of lead: **Aunt Ruth**

Notes: **4/10 called. Anna on vacation. Call back 4/15. 4/15 Interview set 4/20 at 1:30. 4/20 Anna showed me around. They use the same computers we used in school. Sent thank-you note and JIST Card. Call back 5/1. 5/1 Second interview 5/8 at 9 a.m.**

Maintain a Job Search Follow-Up Box

As you contact more and more people in your job search, the number of job lead cards you create for future follow-up will increase. You will get more and more new leads as you follow up with people you've contacted one or more times in the past. You need a way to organize all those job lead cards.

Most department and office supply stores sell small file boxes for 3-by-5-inch cards, as well as tabbed dividers for these boxes. Everything you need will cost about $10.

Set up file box dividers for each day of the month, numbering them 1 through 31. Then, file each completed job lead card under the date when you want to follow up on it.

Every Monday, simply review all the job lead cards filed for the week. On your weekly schedule, list any interviews or follow-up calls you promised to make at a particular date and time. At the start of each day, pull the job lead cards filed under that date. List appointments and calls on your Daily Job Search Contact Sheet (described in the next section).

Seven Steps to Getting a Job Fast

Keep Trying

Here are some other ways you can use this simple follow-up system to get results:

- ◆ You get the name of a person to call, but you can't reach this person right away. Create a job lead card and file it under tomorrow's date.

- ◆ You call someone from a yellow pages listing, but she is busy this week. She asks you to call back in two weeks. You file this job lead card under the date for two weeks in the future.

- ◆ You get an interview with a person who doesn't have any openings now. He gives you the name of someone who might have an opening. After you send a thank-you note and JIST Card to the original contact, you file his name under a date a few weeks in the future, so that you can check for any future openings.

Following up with past contacts is one of the most effective ways of getting a job! The job search follow-up box is a simple, inexpensive system that works very well. You can do the same thing with computer scheduling software, but it doesn't work any better than the box.

Daily Job Search Contact Sheet

If you do what I suggest, you will try each day to set up 2 interviews. To get this done, you will have to contact a lot of people. Some you will contact for the first time; others you will follow up with from earlier contacts.

To get you started, I suggest that you begin each day by completing a Daily Job Search Contact Sheet. Use it to list at least 20 people or organizations to call. Use any sources to get these leads, including people you know, referrals, yellow pages leads, Internet leads, and want ads. An example of a contact sheet follows.

Quip

Is a computer better than 3-by-5 cards?

Maybe not. If you already use scheduling or time management software, go ahead and use it to manage your job search contacts. If you don't use such software now, you will probably be better off trying the card system I suggest. The reason is simple—it works. Instead of spending your time messing with new software, you can go right to work making contacts and getting results.

Sample Daily Job Search Contact Sheet

Contact Name/ Organization	Referral Source	Job Lead Card?	Phone Number/ E-Mail Address
1. Manager/The Flower Show	Yellow pages	Yes	897-6041
2. Manager/Rainbow Flowers	Listed on Rainbow's Web site	Yes	admin@rainbowflowers.com
3. Joyce Wilson/Hartley Nurseries	John Lee	Yes	892-2224
4. John Mullahy/Roses, Etc.	Uncle Jim	Yes	299-4226
5. None/Plants to Go	Want Ad	Yes	835-7016

In Closing

This is a short book, but it may be all you need to get a better job in less time. I hope this will be true for you and wish you well in your search.

Do remember that you won't get a job offer because someone knocks on your door and offers one. Job seeking does involve luck, but you are more likely to get lucky if you are out getting interviews.

I'll close this book with a few final tips:

- ◆ **Approach your job search as if it were a job itself.**

  Create and stick to a daily schedule, and spend at least 25 hours a week looking.

- ◆ **Follow up on each lead you generate and ask each contact for referrals.**

- ◆ **Set out each day to schedule at least 2 interviews.**

  Use the new definition of an interview, which includes talking to businesses that don't have an opening now.

- ◆ **Send out lots of thank-you notes and JIST Cards.**

- ◆ **When you want the job, tell the employer that you want it and why the company should hire you over someone else.**

Don't get discouraged. There are lots of jobs out there, and someone needs an employee with your skills—your job is to find that someone.

I wish you luck in your job search and in your life.

 *Appendix A*

The Essential Job Search Data Worksheet

Take some time to complete this worksheet carefully. It will help you write your resume and answer interview questions. You can also tear it out and take it with you to help complete applications and as a reference throughout your job search.

Use an erasable pen or pencil to allow for corrections. Whenever possible, emphasize skills and accomplishments that support your ability to do the job you want. Use extra sheets as needed.

ESSENTIAL JOB SEARCH DATA WORKSHEET

Your name _____

Date completed _____

Job objective _____

_____

_____

Key Accomplishments

List three accomplishments that best prove your ability to do the kind of job you want.

1. _____

2. _____

3. _____

(continues)

(continued)

Education and Training

Name of high school(s); years attended _____

_____

_____

Subjects related to job objective_____

_____

_____

_____

_____

Related extracurricular activities/hobbies/leisure activities _____

_____

_____

_____

_____

Accomplishments/things you did well _____

_____

_____

_____

_____

Specific things you can do as a result _____

_____

_____

_____

_____

Schools you attended after high school; years attended; degrees/
certificates earned _____

_____

_____

_____

_____

Courses related to job objective _____

_____

_____

_____

_____

Related extracurricular activities/hobbies/leisure activities _____

_____

_____

_____

_____

Accomplishments/things you did well _____

_____

_____

_____

_____

Specific things you can do as a result _____

_____

_____

_____

_____

(continues)

(continued)

Other Training

Include formal or informal learning, workshops, military training, things you learned on-the-job or from hobbies—anything that will help support your job objective. Include specific dates, certificates earned, or other details as needed. _____

_____

_____

_____

_____

Work and Volunteer History

List your most recent job first, followed by each previous job. Military experience, unpaid or volunteer work, and work in a family business should be included here, too. If needed, use additional sheets to cover *all* significant paid or unpaid work experiences.

Emphasize details that will help support your new job objective! Include numbers to support what you did: number of people served over one or more years, number of transactions processed, percentage of sales increased, total inventory value you were responsible for, payroll of the staff you supervised, total budget responsible for, and so on.

Emphasize results you achieved, using numbers to support them whenever possible. Mentioning these things on your resume and in an interview will help you get the job you want!

Job 1

Dates employed _____

_____

Name of organization _____

_____

Supervisor's name and job title _____

_____

Address _____

_____

_____

_____

Phone number/e-mail address/Web site _____

_____

_____

What did you accomplish and do well? _____

_____

_____

_____

Things you learned, skills you developed or used _____

_____

_____

_____

Raises, promotions, positive evaluations, awards _____

_____

_____

_____

_____

Computer software, hardware, and other equipment you used

_____

_____

_____

_____

(continues)

(continued)

Other details that might support your job objective _____

_____

_____

_____

_____

Job 2

Dates employed _____

_____

Name of organization _____

_____

Supervisor's name and job title _____

_____

Address _____

_____

_____

_____

Phone number/e-mail address/Web site _____

_____

_____

What did you accomplish and do well? _____

_____

_____

_____

_____

Things you learned, skills you developed or used _____

_____

_____

_____

_____

Raises, promotions, positive evaluations, awards _____

_____

_____

_____

_____

Computer software, hardware, and other equipment you used

_____

_____

_____

_____

Other details that might support your job objective _____

_____

_____

_____

_____

Job 3

Dates employed_____

_____

Name of organization _____

_____

(continues)

(continued)

Supervisor's name and job title _____

_____

Address _____

_____

_____

_____

Phone number/e-mail address/Web site_____

_____

_____

What did you accomplish and do well? _____

_____

_____

_____

_____

Things you learned, skills you developed or used _____

_____

_____

_____

_____

Raises, promotions, positive evaluations, awards _____

_____

_____

_____

Computer software, hardware, and other equipment you used

_____

_____

_____

_____

Other details that might support your job objective _____

_____

_____

_____

_____

References

Think of people who know your work well and will say positive things about your work and character. Past supervisors are best.

Contact them and tell them what type of job you want and your qualifications, and ask what they will say about you if contacted by a potential employer. Some employers will not provide references by phone, so ask them for a letter of reference for you in advance.

If a past employer may say negative things, negotiate what they will say or get written references from others you worked with there.

Reference name _____

_____

Position or title _____

_____

Relationship to you _____

_____

(continues)

(continued)

Contact information (complete address, phone number, e-mail address _____

_____

_____

_____

_____

Reference name _____

_____

Position or title _____

_____

Relationship to you _____

_____

Contact information (complete address, phone number, e-mail address _____

_____

_____

_____

_____

Reference name _____

_____

Position or title _____

_____

Relationship to you _____

_____

Contact information (complete address, phone number, e-mail address _____

_____

_____

_____

_____

Sample Job Description from the Occupational Outlook Handbook

The following is an example of one of the many job descriptions that can be found in the *Occupational Outlook Handbook,* compiled by the U.S. Department of Labor. Reviewing *OOH* job descriptions will help you match your skills to jobs that interest you and will introduce you to the powerful skills language that draws employers' attention.

The *OOH* can be found in most libraries, as well as on the Internet at the Web site stats.bls.gov/oco/home.htm. The *OOH* is updated every two years, so make sure you are using a current edition so that you get the most recent information available.

Management and Business and Financial Operations Occupations

Accountants and Auditors

Significant Points

- Most jobs require at least a bachelor's degree in accounting or a related field.

- Job seekers who obtain professional recognition through certification or licensure, a master's degree, proficiency in accounting and auditing computer software, or specialized expertise will have an advantage in the job market.

- Competition will remain keen for the most prestigious jobs in major accounting and business firms.

Nature of the Work

Accountants and auditors help to ensure that the nation's firms are run more efficiently, its public records kept more accurately, and its taxes paid properly and on time. They perform these vital functions by offering an increasingly wide array of business and accounting services to their clients. These services include public, management, and government accounting, as well as internal auditing. However, accountants and auditors are broadening the services they offer to include budget analysis, financial and investment planning, information technology consulting, and limited legal services. Beyond the fundamental tasks of the occupation—preparing, analyzing, and verifying financial documents in order to provide information to clients—many accountants now are required to possess a wide range of knowledge and skills.

Specific job duties vary widely among the four major fields of accounting. *Public accountants* perform a broad range of accounting, auditing, tax, and consulting activities for their clients, who may be corporations, governments, nonprofit organizations, or individuals. For example, some public accountants concentrate on tax matters, such as advising companies of the tax advantages and disadvantages of certain business decisions and preparing individual income tax returns. Others are consultants who offer advice in areas such as compensation or employee healthcare benefits, the design of accounting and data processing systems, and the selection of controls to safeguard assets. Some specialize in forensic accounting—investigating and interpreting bankruptcies and other complex financial transactions. Still others audit clients' financial statements and report to investors and authorities that the statements have been correctly prepared and reported. Public accountants, many of whom are Certified Public Accountants (CPAs), generally have their own businesses or work for public accounting firms.

Management accountants—also called industrial, corporate, or private accountants—record and analyze the financial information of the companies for which they work. Other responsibilities include budgeting, performance evaluation, cost management, and asset management. Usually, management accountants are part of executive teams involved in strategic planning or new-product development. They analyze and interpret the financial information that corporate executives need to make sound business decisions. They also prepare financial reports for non-management groups, including stockholders, creditors, regulatory agencies, and tax authorities. Within accounting departments, they may work in various areas including financial analysis, planning and budgeting, and cost accounting.

Many persons with an accounting background work in the public sector. *Government accountants and auditors* maintain and examine the records of government agencies and audit private businesses and individuals whose activities are subject to government regulations or taxation. Accountants employed by federal, state, and local governments guarantee that revenues are received and expenditures are made in accordance with laws and regulations. Those who are employed by the federal government may work as Internal Revenue Service agents or in financial management, financial institution examination, or budget analysis and administration.

Internal auditing is an increasingly important area of accounting and auditing. *Internal auditors* verify the accuracy of their organization's records and check for mismanagement, waste, or fraud. Specifically, they examine and evaluate their firms' financial and information systems, management procedures, and internal controls to ensure that records are accurate and controls are adequate to protect against fraud and waste. They also review company operations—evaluating their efficiency, effectiveness, and compliance with corporate policies and procedures, laws, and government regulations. There are many types of highly specialized auditors, such as electronic data processing, environmental, engineering, legal, insurance premium, bank, and healthcare auditors. As computer systems make information more timely, internal auditors help managers to base their decisions on actual data, rather than personal observation. Internal auditors also may recommend controls for their organization's computer system to ensure the reliability of the system and the integrity of the data.

Computers are rapidly changing the nature of the work for most accountants and auditors. With the aid of special software packages, accountants summarize transactions in standard formats for financial records and organize data in special formats for financial analysis. These accounting packages greatly reduce the amount of tedious manual work associated with data management and recordkeeping. Personal and laptop computers enable accountants and auditors to be more mobile and to use their clients' computer systems to extract information from large mainframe computers. As a result, a growing number of accountants and auditors have extensive computer skills and specialize in correcting problems with software or in developing software to meet unique data management and analytical needs. Accountants also are beginning to perform more technical duties, such as implementing, controlling, and auditing systems and networks, and developing technology plans and budgets.

Accountants also are increasingly assuming the role of a personal financial advisor. They not only provide clients with accounting and tax help, but also help them develop a personal budget, manage assets and investments, plan for retirement, and recognize and reduce exposure to risks. This role is a response to demands by clients for one trustworthy individual or firm to meet all of their financial needs.

Working Conditions

Most accountants and auditors work in a typical office setting. Self-employed accountants may be able to do part of their work at home. Accountants and auditors employed by public accounting firms and government agencies may travel frequently to perform audits at branches of their firm, clients' places of business, or government facilities.

Most accountants and auditors generally work a standard 40-hour week, but many work longer hours, particularly if they are self-employed and have numerous clients. Tax specialists often work long hours during the tax season.

Employment

Accountants and auditors held about 976,000 jobs in 2000. They worked throughout private industry and government, but almost 1 out of 4 salaried accountants worked for accounting, auditing, and bookkeeping firms. Approximately 3 out of 25 accountants or auditors were self-employed.

Many accountants and auditors are unlicensed management accountants, internal auditors, or government accountants and auditors; however, a large number are licensed Certified Public Accountants. Most accountants and auditors work in urban areas, where public accounting firms and central or regional offices of businesses are concentrated.

Some individuals with backgrounds in accounting and auditing are full-time college and university faculty; others teach part-time while working as self-employed accountants or as salaried accountants for private industry or government.

Training, Other Qualifications, and Advancement

Most accountant and internal auditor positions require at least a bachelor's degree in accounting or a related field. Beginning accounting and auditing positions in the federal government, for example, usually require four years of college (including 24 semester hours in accounting or auditing) or an equivalent combination of education and experience. Some employers prefer applicants with a master's degree in accounting or with a master's degree in business administration with a concentration in accounting.

Previous experience in accounting or auditing can help an applicant get a job. Many colleges offer students an opportunity to gain experience through summer or part-time internship programs conducted by public accounting or business firms. In addition, practical knowledge of computers and their applications in accounting and internal auditing is a great asset for job seekers in the accounting field.

Professional recognition through certification or licensure provides a distinct advantage in the job market. All CPAs must have a certificate, and any partners in their firm must have licenses issued by a state Board of Accountancy. The vast majority of states require CPA candidates to be college graduates, but a few states substitute a number of years of public accounting experience for a college degree. Based on recommendations made by the American Institute of Certified Public Accountants, 38 states currently require CPA candidates to complete 150 semester hours of college coursework —an additional 30 hours beyond the usual 4-year bachelor's degree. Most states have adopted similar legislation that will become effective in the future. Many schools have altered their curricula accordingly, and prospective accounting majors should carefully research accounting curricula and the requirements of any states in which they hope to become licensed.

All states use the four-part Uniform CPA Examination prepared by the American Institute of Certified Public Accountants (AICPA). The 2-day CPA examination is rigorous, and only about one-quarter of those who take it each year passes every part they attempt. Candidates are not required to pass all four parts at once, but most states require candidates to pass at least two parts for partial credit and to complete all four sections within a certain period. Most states also require applicants for a CPA certificate to have some accounting experience.

The AICPA also offers members with valid CPA certificates the option to receive the Accredited in Business Valuation (ABV), Certified Information Technology Professional (CITP), or Personal Financial Specialist (PFS) designations. The addition of these designations to the CPA distinguishes those accountants with a certain level of expertise in the nontraditional areas of business valuation, technology, or personal financial planning, in which accountants are practicing more frequently. The ABV designation requires a written exam, as well as completion of a minimum of 10 business valuation projects that demonstrate a candidate's experience and competence. The CITP requires payment of a fee, a written statement of intent, and the achievement of a set number of points awarded for business experience and education. Those who do not meet the required number of points may substitute a written exam. Candidates for the PFS designation also must achieve a certain level of points, based on experience and education, and must pass a written exam and submit references, as well.

Nearly all states require CPAs and other public accountants to complete a certain number of hours of continuing professional education before their licenses can be renewed. The professional associations representing accountants sponsor numerous courses, seminars, group study programs, and other forms of continuing education.

Accountants and auditors also can seek to obtain other forms of credentials from professional societies on a voluntary basis. Voluntary certification can attest to professional competence in a specialized field of accounting and auditing. It also can certify that a recognized level of professional competence has been achieved by accountants and auditors who acquired some skills on the job, without the formal education or public accounting work experience needed to meet the rigorous standards required to take the CPA examination.

The Institute of Management Accountants (IMA) confers the Certified Management Accountant (CMA) designation upon applicants who complete a bachelor's degree or attain a minimum score on specified graduate school entrance exams. Applicants also must pass a four-part examination, agree to meet continuing education requirements, comply with standards of professional conduct, and have worked at least 2 years in management accounting. The CMA program is administered by the Institute of Certified Management Accountants, an affiliate of the IMA.

Graduates from accredited colleges and universities who have worked for 2 years as internal auditors and have passed a four-part examination may earn the Certified Internal Auditor (CIA) designation from the Institute of Internal Auditors. Similarly, the Information Systems Audit and Control Association confers the Certified Information Systems Auditor (CISA) designation upon candidates who pass an examination and have 5 years of experience in auditing electronic data-processing systems. Auditing or data processing experience and college education may be substituted for up to 2 years of work experience in this program. The Accreditation Council for Accountancy and Taxation, a satellite organization of the National Society of Public Accountants, confers three designations—Accredited in Accountancy (AA), Accredited Tax Advisor (ATA), and Accredited Tax Preparer (ATP). Candidates for the AA must pass an exam, while candidates for the ATA and ATP must complete the required coursework and pass an exam. Often, a practitioner will hold multiple licenses and designations. For instance, an internal auditor might be a CPA, CIA, and CISA.

The Association of Government Accountants grants the Certified Government Financial Manager (CGFM) designation for accountants, auditors, and other government financial personnel at the federal, state, and local levels. Candidates must have a minimum of a bachelor's degree, 24 hours of study in financial management, and 2 years' experience in government, and must pass a series of three exams. The exams cover topics in governmental environment; governmental accounting, financial reporting, and budgeting; and financial management and control.

Persons planning a career in accounting should have an aptitude for mathematics and be able to analyze, compare, and interpret facts and figures quickly. They must be able to clearly communicate the results of their work to clients and managers. Accountants and auditors must be good at working with people, as well as with business systems and computers. Because millions of financial statement users rely on their services, accountants and auditors should have high standards of integrity.

Capable accountants and auditors may advance rapidly; those having inadequate academic preparation may be assigned routine jobs and find promotion difficult. Many graduates of junior colleges and business and correspondence schools, as well as bookkeepers and accounting clerks who meet the education and experience requirements set by their employers, can obtain junior accounting positions and advance to positions with more responsibilities by demonstrating their accounting skills on the job.

Beginning public accountants usually start by assisting with work for several clients. They may advance to positions with more responsibility in 1 or 2 years, and to senior positions within another few years. Those who excel may become supervisors, managers, or partners; open their own public accounting firms; or transfer to executive positions in management accounting or internal auditing in private firms.

Management accountants often start as cost accountants, junior internal auditors, or trainees for other accounting positions. As they rise through the organization, they may advance to accounting manager, chief cost accountant, budget director, or manager of internal auditing. Some become controllers, treasurers, financial vice presidents, chief financial officers, or corporation presidents. Many senior corporation executives have a background in accounting, internal auditing, or finance.

In general, public accountants, management accountants, and internal auditors have much occupational mobility. Practitioners often shift into management accounting or internal auditing from public accounting, or between internal auditing and management accounting. However, it is less common for accountants and auditors to move from either management accounting or internal auditing into public accounting.

Job Outlook

Accountants and auditors who have earned professional recognition through certification or licensure should have the best job prospects. For example, Certified Public Accountants should continue to enjoy a wide range of job opportunities, especially as more states require candidates to have 150 hours of college coursework, making it more difficult to obtain this certification. Similarly, Certified Management Accountants should be in demand as their management advice is increasingly sought. Applicants with a master's degree in accounting, or a master's degree in business administration with a concentration in accounting, also will have an advantage in the job market.

Proficiency in accounting and auditing computer software, or expertise in specialized areas such as international business, specific industries, or current legislation, also may be helpful in landing certain accounting and auditing jobs. In addition, employers increasingly seek applicants with strong interpersonal and communication skills. Because many accountants work on teams with others from different backgrounds, they must be able to communicate accounting and financial information clearly and concisely. Regardless of one's qualifications, however, competition will remain keen for the most prestigious jobs in major accounting and business firms.

Employment of accountants and auditors is expected to grow about as fast as the average for all occupations through the year 2010. In addition to openings resulting from growth, the need to replace accountants and auditors who retire or transfer to other occupations will produce numerous job openings annually in this large occupation.

As the economy grows, the number of business establishments will increase, requiring more accountants and auditors to set up books, prepare taxes, and provide management advice. As these businesses grow, the volume and complexity of information developed by accountants and auditors regarding costs, expenditures, and taxes will increase as well. More-complex requirements for accountants and auditors also arise from changes in legislation related to taxes, financial reporting standards, business investments, mergers, and other financial matters. The growth of international business also has led to more demand for accounting expertise and services related to international trade and accounting rules, as well as to international mergers and acquisitions. These trends should create more jobs for accountants and auditors.

The changing role of accountants and auditors also will spur job growth. In response to market demand, these financial specialists will offer more financial management and consulting services as they take on a greater advisory role and develop more-sophisticated and flexible accounting systems. By focusing on analyzing operations, rather than simply providing financial data, accountants will help to boost demand for their services. Also, internal auditors will increasingly be needed to discover and eliminate waste and fraud.

However, these trends will be offset somewhat by a decrease in the demand for traditional services and by the growing use of accounting software. Accountants will spend less time performing audits, due to potential liability and relatively low profits, and will shift away from tax preparation, due to the increasing popularity of tax preparation firms and software. As computer programs continue to simplify some accounting-related tasks, clerical staff will increasingly handle many routine calculations.

Earnings

In 2000, the median annual earnings of accountants and auditors were $43,500. The middle half of the occupation earned between $34,290 and $56,190. The top 10 percent of accountants and auditors earned more than $73,770, and the bottom 10 percent earned less than $28,190. In 2000, median annual earnings in the industries employing the largest numbers of accountants and auditors were

Computer and data processing services	$47,110
Accounting, auditing, and bookkeeping	45,890
Federal government	44,380
Local government	41,240
State government	40,780

According to a salary survey conducted by the National Association of Colleges and Employers, bachelor's degree candidates in accounting received starting offers averaging $39,397 a year in 2001; master's degree candidates in accounting were initially offered $43,272.

According to a 2001 salary survey conducted by Robert Half International, a staffing services firm specializing in accounting and finance, accountants and auditors with up to 1 year of experience earned between $29,250 and $40,250. Those with 1 to 3 years of experience earned between $33,500 and $47,750. Senior accountants and auditors earned between $39,250 and $59,500; managers earned between $46,750 and $76,750; and directors of accounting and auditing earned between $60,500 and $106,500 a year. The variation in salaries reflects differences in size of firm, location, level of education, and professional credentials.

In the federal government, the starting annual salary for junior accountants and auditors was $21,947 in 2001. Candidates who had a superior academic record might start at $27,185, while applicants with a master's degree or 2 years of professional experience usually began at $33,254. Beginning salaries were slightly higher in selected areas where the prevailing local pay level was higher. Accountants employed by the federal government in nonsupervisory, supervisory, and managerial positions averaged $64,770 a year in 2001; auditors averaged $67,180.

Related Occupations

Accountants and auditors design internal control systems and analyze financial data. Others for whom training in accounting is invaluable include budget analysts; cost estimators; loan officers; financial analysts and personal financial advisors; tax examiners, collectors, and revenue agents; bill and account collectors; and bookkeeping, accounting, and auditing clerks. Recently, accountants increasingly have taken on the role of management analysts.

Sources of Additional Information

Information about careers in certified public accounting and CPA standards and examinations may be obtained from the following:

♦ American Institute of Certified Public Accountants
1211 Avenue of the Americas
New York, NY 10036
Internet: www.aicpa.org

Information on CPA licensure requirements by state may be obtained from the following:

- ◆ National Association of State Boards of Accountancy
  150 Fourth Ave. North
  Suite 700
  Nashville, TN 37219-2417
  Internet: www.nasba.org

Information on careers in management accounting and the CMA designation may be obtained from the following:

- ◆ Institute of Management Accountants
  10 Paragon Dr.
  Montvale, NJ 07645-1760
  Internet: www.imanet.org

Information on the Accredited in Accountancy, Accredited Business Accountant, Accredited Tax Advisor, or Accredited Tax Preparer designations may be obtained from the following:

- ◆ Accreditation Council for Accountancy and Taxation
  1010 N. Fairfax St.
  Alexandria, VA 22314
  Internet: www.acatcredentials.org

Information on careers in internal auditing and the CIA designation may be obtained from the following:

- ◆ The Institute of Internal Auditors
  249 Maitland Ave.
  Altamonte Springs, FL 32701-4201
  Internet: www.theiia.org

Information on careers in information systems auditing and the CISA designation may be obtained from the following:

- ◆ The Information Systems Audit and Control Association
  3701 Algonquin Rd.
  Suite 1010
  Rolling Meadows, IL 60008
  Internet: www.isaca.org

Information on careers in government accounting and on the CGFM designation may be obtained from the following:

◆ Association of Government Accountants
2208 Mount Vernon Ave.
Alexandria, VA 22301
Internet: www.agacgfm.org

Information on obtaining an accounting position with the federal government is available from the Office of Personnel Management (OPM) through a telephone-based system. Consult your telephone directory under U.S. Government for a local number or call (912) 757-3000; Federal Relay Service: (800) 877-8339.

The first number is not toll free, and charges may result. Information also is available from the OPM Internet site: www.usajobs.opm.gov.

O*NET Codes

13-2011.01, 13-2011.02

A Short List of Additional Resources

Thousands of books and uncounted Internet sites provide information on career subjects. Space limitations do not permit me to describe the many good resources available, so I list here some of the most useful ones. Because this is my list, I've included books I've written or that JIST publishes. You should be able to find these and many other resources at libraries, bookstores, and Web book-selling sites, such as Amazon.com.

Resumes and Cover Letter Books

My books. I'm told that *The Quick Resume & Cover Letter Book* is now one of the top-selling resume books at various large bookstore chains. It is very simple to follow, is inexpensive, has good design, and has good sample resumes written by professional resume writers. *America's Top Resumes for America's Top Jobs* includes a wonderfully diverse collection of resumes covering most major jobs and life situations, plus brief but helpful resume-writing advice.

Other books published by JIST. The following titles include many sample resumes written by professional resume writers, as well as good advice: *Cover Letter Magic,* Enelow and Kursmark; *Cyberspace Resume Kit,* Nemnich and Jandt; *The Edge Resume & Job Search Strategy,* Corbin and Wright; *The Federal Resume Guidebook,* Troutman; *Expert Resumes for Computer and Web Jobs,* Enelow and Kursmark; *Expert Resumes for Teachers and Educators,* Enelow and Kursmark; *Expert Resumes for Manufacturing Careers,* Enelow and Kursmark; *Gallery of Best Cover Letters,* Noble; *Gallery of Best Resumes,* Noble; *Gallery of Best Resumes for People Without a Four-Year Degree,* Noble; and *Résumé Magic,* Whitcomb.

Job Search Books

My books. *The Very Quick Job Search—Get a Better Job in Half the Time* is a thorough book with detailed advice and a "quick" section of key tips you can finish in a few hours. *The Quick Interview & Salary Negotiation Book* also has a section of quick tips likely to make the biggest difference in your job search, as well as sections with more detailed information on problem questions and other topics. *Getting the Job You Really Want* includes many in-the-book activities and good career decision-making and job search advice.

Other books published by JIST. Titles include *Career Success Is Color Blind*, Stevenson; *Cyberspace Job Search Kit*, Nemnich and Jandt; *Inside Secrets to Finding a Teaching Job*, Warner and Bryan; and *Job Search Handbook for People with Disabilities*.

Books with Information on Jobs

Primary references. The *Occupational Outlook Handbook* is the source of job titles listed in this book. Published by the U.S. Department of Labor and updated every other year, the OOH covers about 85 percent of the workforce. A book titled the *O*NET Dictionary of Occupational Titles* has descriptions for over 1,000 jobs based on the O*NET (for Occupational Information Network) database developed by the Department of Labor. The *Enhanced Occupational Outlook Handbook* includes the OOH descriptions plus more than 2,000 additional descriptions of related jobs from the O*NET and other sources. The *Guide for Occupational Exploration,* Third Edition, allows you to explore major jobs based on your interests. All of these books are available from JIST.

Other books published by JIST. Here are a few good books that include job descriptions and helpful details on career options: *America's Fastest Growing Jobs; America's Top Jobs for College Graduates; America's Top Jobs for People Without a Four-Year Degree; America's Top Computer and Technical Jobs; America's Top Medical, Education & Human Services Jobs; America's Top White-Collar Jobs; Best Jobs for the 21st Century* (plus versions for people with and without degrees); *Career Guide to America's Top Industries; and Guide to America's Federal Jobs*.

Internet Resources

If the Internet is new to you, I recommend a book titled *Cyberspace Job Search Kit* by Mary Nemnich and Fred Jandt. It covers the basics plus offers advice on using the Internet for career planning and job seeking. The *Quick Internet Guide to Career and Education Information* by Anne Wolfinger gives excellent reviews of the most helpful sites and ideas on how to use them. The *Occupational Outlook Handbook*'s job descriptions also include Internet addresses. And www.jist.com lists recommended sites for career, education, and related topics, along with comments on each.

Be aware that some sites provide poor advice, so ask your librarian, instructor, or counselor for suggestions on those best for your needs.

Other Resources

Libraries. Most libraries have the books mentioned here, as well as many other resources. Many also provide Internet access so that you can research online information. Ask the librarian for help finding what you need.

People. People who hold the jobs that interest you are one of the best career information sources. Ask them what they like and don't like about their work, how they got started, and the education or training needed. Most people are helpful and will give advice you can't get any other way.

Career counseling. A good vocational counselor can help you explore career options. Take advantage of this service if it is available to you! Also consider a career-planning course or program, which will encourage you to be more thorough in your thinking.

Index

help-wanted ads, 41
honesty on resumes, 68

I

ideal jobs. *See* objectives
industries, 34–37
information and record clerks, 29
installation, maintenance, and repair
  occupations, 31–32
insurance industries, 36
interests, listing on worksheets, 37
Internet
  employment agencies, 42
  help-wanted ads, 41
  job search methods, 64–66
  resume posting, 44, 65–66
  resumes, 77
  yellow pages, 50
interviews
  college graduates, 109
  cover letters, 88
  grooming, 105
  improving, 2
  preparation, 107–109
  professionalism, 106
  questions, 107–109
  resumes, 69
  salary negotiations, 109–111
  scheduling, 1, 101
inventory. *See* skills, assessment

J

JIST Cards
  career change, 54
  college graduates, 54
  combination resumes, 96–97
  education, 53, 58, 60
  good worker traits, 53, 62
  job search methods, 51–62
  job-related skills, 53
  military service, 55
  objectives, 53, 57
  personal information, 52–53, 56
  phone calls, 63–64
  skills, 61–62

special working conditions, 62
training, 53, 58, 60–61
transferable skills, 55
volunteer experience, 58
work experience, 53, 56–59
worksheets, 56–63
JIST Web site, 66
job descriptions, *Occupational Outlook
  Handbook (OOH),* 80, 131–142
  advancement opportunities, 134–138
  education requirements, 134–138
  employment statistics, 134
  nature of the work, 132–134
  O*NET codes, 142
  outlook, 138–139
  related jobs, 140
  salary, 139–140
  training requirements, 134–138
  working conditions, 134
job search methods
  applications, 39, 41–42
  contacting employers directly, 39–42, 51
  daily job search contact sheet, 116–117
  daily schedules, 102–104
  effectiveness, 40
  employment agencies, 42–43
  friends/relatives, 39
  help-wanted ads, 39, 41
  Internet, 44, 64–66
  JIST Cards, 51, 62
    career change, 54
    college graduates, 54
    education, 53
    good worker traits, 53
    job-related skills, 53
    military service, 55
    objectives, 53
    personal information, 52–53
    training, 53
    transferable skills, 55
    work experience, 53, 56
  job lead cards, 114–115
  job search follow-up box, 115–116
  networking, 44–48
  phone calls, 50

K–L

M

N

O

O*NET codes, 142
office and administrative support
occupations, 28–29
production occupations, 32–33
professional and related occupations, 22–26
related jobs, 140
salary, 139–140
sales and related occupations, 28
service occupations, 27–28
training requirements, 134–138
transportation and material moving
occupations, 33–34
working conditions, 134
occupations
researching, 19–20
worksheets, 37
office and administrative support occupations, 28–30
OOH. *See Occupational Outlook Handbook (OOH)*
organizational skills, 10
outlook. *See Occupational Outlook Handbook (OOH)*

P

paper resumes
quality of, 77
reformatting, 82
pay. *See* salary
people skills, 10–11
personal care and service occupations, 27
personal information
chronological resumes, 70–74
combination resumes, 78–79
electronic resumes, 81
JIST Cards, 52–53, 56
phone calls to potential employers, 50, 63–64
physical environment, listed in objectives, 16
physical scientist occupations, 25
plant and system operators, 32
pocket schedulers, 114
Postal Service occupations, 30
preparation for interviews, 107–109
printing occupations, 33
printing resumes, 68

private employment agencies, 39, 43
production occupations, 32–33
professional and related occupations, 22–26
Professional Association of Résumé Writers and Career Coaches, 91
professional organizations, using for job searches, 39
professionalism in interviews, 106
promotions, chronological resumes, 75
protective service occupations, 28
public employment agencies, 39
public utilities occupations, 35

Q–R

questions during interview, 107–109

record clerk occupations, 29
references
chronological resumes, 72–74
combination resumes, 78–79
electronic resumes, 81
worksheets, 127–129
referrals, 47, 115
reformatting paper resumes, 82
related jobs in *Occupational Outlook Handbook (OOH)*, 140
related skills, objectives, 15–16
relatives. *See* networking
repair occupations, 31–32
research skills, 11, 19–20
responsibilities, listed with objectives, 17
results. *See* accomplishments
resumes
accomplishments, 68, 93
chronological
accomplishments, 74
addresses, 70–71
contact information, 70–71
education, 71–74
gaps in employment, 75
job titles, 74
names, 70–71
objectives, 71–74
personal information, 72–74
promotions, 75